Architecture: A Very Short Introduction

VERY SHORT INTRODUCTIONS are for anyone wanting a stimulating and accessible way in to a new subject. They are written by experts, and have been published in more than 25 languages worldwide.

The series began in 1995, and now represents a wide variety of topics in history, philosophy, religion, science, and the humanities. Over the next few years it will grow to a library of around 200 volumes – a Very Short Introduction to everything from ancient Egypt and Indian philosophy to conceptual art and cosmology.

Very Short Introductions available now:

ANCIENT PHILOSOPHY Julia Annas
THE ANGLO-SAXON AGE John Blair
ANIMAL RIGHTS David DeGrazia
ARCHAEOLOGY Paul Bahn
ARCHITECTURE Andrew Ballantyne
ARISTOTLE Jonathan Barnes
ART HISTORY Dana Arnold
ART THEORY Cynthia Freeland
THE HISTORY OF ASTRONOMY Michael Hoskin
ATHEISM Julian Baggini
AUGUSTINE Henry Chadwick
BARTHES Jonathan Culler
THE BIBLE John Riches
BRITISH POLITICS Anthony Wright
BUDDHA Michael Carrithers
BUDDHISM Damien Keown
CAPITALISM James Fulcher
THE CELTS Barry Cunliffe
CHOICE THEORY Michael Allingham
CHRISTIAN ART Beth Williamson
CLASSICS Mary Beard and John Henderson
CLAUSEWITZ Michael Howard
THE COLD WAR Robert McMahon
CONTINENTAL PHILOSOPHY Simon Critchley
COSMOLOGY Peter Coles
CRYPTOGRAPHY Fred Piper and Sean Murphy
DADA AND SURREALISM David Hopkins
DARWIN Jonathan Howard
DEMOCRACY Bernard Crick
DESCARTES Tom Sorell
DRUGS Leslie Iversen
THE EARTH Martin Redfern
EGYPTIAN MYTHOLOGY Geraldine Pinch
EIGHTEENTH-CENTURY BRITAIN Paul Langford
THE ELEMENTS Philip Ball
EMOTION Dylan Evans
EMPIRE Stephen Howe
ENGELS Terrell Carver
ETHICS Simon Blackburn
THE EUROPEAN UNION John Pinder
EVOLUTION Brian and Deborah Charlesworth
FASCISM Kevin Passmore
THE FRENCH REVOLUTION William Doyle
FREUD Anthony Storr
GALILEO Stillman Drake
GANDHI Bhikhu Parekh

GLOBALIZATION Manfred Steger
HEGEL Peter Singer
HEIDEGGER Michael Inwood
HINDUISM Kim Knott
HISTORY John H. Arnold
HOBBES Richard Tuck
HUME A. J. Ayer
IDEOLOGY Michael Freeden
INDIAN PHILOSOPHY Sue Hamilton
INTELLIGENCE Ian J. Deary
ISLAM Malise Ruthven
JUDAISM Norman Solomon
JUNG Anthony Stevens
KANT Roger Scruton
KIERKEGAARD Patrick Gardiner
THE KORAN Michael Cook
LINGUISTICS Peter Matthews
LITERARY THEORY Jonathan Culler
LOCKE John Dunn
LOGIC Graham Priest
MACHIAVELLI Quentin Skinner
MARX Peter Singer
MATHEMATICS Timothy Gowers
MEDIEVAL BRITAIN John Gillingham and Ralph A. Griffiths
MODERN IRELAND Senia Pašeta
MOLECULES Philip Ball
MUSIC Nicholas Cook
NIETZSCHE Michael Tanner
NINETEENTH-CENTURY BRITAIN Christopher Harvie and H. C. G. Matthew
NORTHERN IRELAND Marc Mulholland
PAUL E. P. Sanders
PHILOSOPHY Edward Craig
PHILOSOPHY OF SCIENCE Samir Okasha
PLATO Julia Annas
POLITICS Kenneth Minogue
POLITICAL PHILOSOPHY David Miller
POSTCOLONIALISM Robert Young
POSTMODERNISM Christopher Butler
POSTSTRUCTURALISM Catherine Belsey
PREHISTORY Chris Gosden
PRESOCRATIC PHILOSOPHY Catherine Osborne
PSYCHOLOGY Gillian Butler and Freda McManus
QUANTUM THEORY John Polkinghorne
ROMAN BRITAIN Peter Salway
ROUSSEAU Robert Wokler
RUSSELL A. C. Grayling
RUSSIAN LITERATURE Catriona Kelly
THE RUSSIAN REVOLUTION S. A. Smith
SCHIZOPHRENIA Chris Frith and Eve Johnstone
SCHOPENHAUER Christopher Janaway
SHAKESPEARE Germaine Greer
SOCIAL AND CULTURAL ANTHROPOLOGY John Monaghan and Peter Just
SOCIOLOGY Steve Bruce
SOCRATES C. C. W. Taylor
SPINOZA Roger Scruton
STUART BRITAIN John Morrill
TERRORISM Charles Townshend
THEOLOGY David F. Ford
THE TUDORS John Guy
TWENTIETH-CENTURY BRITAIN Kenneth O. Morgan
WITTGENSTEIN A. C. Grayling
WORLD MUSIC Philip Bohlman

Available soon:

AFRICAN HISTORY
John Parker and Richard Rathbone
ANCIENT EGYPT Ian Shaw
THE BRAIN Michael O'Shea
BUDDHIST ETHICS
Damien Keown
CHAOS Leonard Smith
CHRISTIANITY Linda Woodhead
CITIZENSHIP Richard Bellamy
CLASSICAL ARCHITECTURE
Robert Tavernor
CLONING Arlene Judith Klotzko
CONTEMPORARY ART
Julian Stallabrass
THE CRUSADES
Christopher Tyerman
DERRIDA Simon Glendinning
DESIGN John Heskett
DINOSAURS David Norman
DREAMING J. Allan Hobson
ECONOMICS Partha Dasgupta
THE END OF THE WORLD
Bill McGuire
EXISTENTIALISM Thomas Flynn
THE FIRST WORLD WAR
Michael Howard
FREE WILL Thomas Pink
FUNDAMENTALISM
Malise Ruthven
HABERMAS Gordon Finlayson
HIEROGLYPHS
Penelope Wilson
HIROSHIMA B. R. Tomlinson
HUMAN EVOLUTION
Bernard Wood
INTERNATIONAL RELATIONS
Paul Wilkinson
JAZZ Brian Morton
MANDELA Tom Lodge
MEDICAL ETHICS
Tony Hope
THE MIND Martin Davies
MYTH Robert Segal
NATIONALISM Steven Grosby
PERCEPTION Richard Gregory
PHILOSOPHY OF RELIGION
Jack Copeland and Diane Proudfoot
PHOTOGRAPHY
Steve Edwards
THE RAJ Denis Judd
THE RENAISSANCE
Jerry Brotton
RENAISSANCE ART
Geraldine Johnson
SARTRE Christina Howells
THE SPANISH CIVIL WAR
Helen Graham
TRAGEDY Adrian Poole
THE TWENTIETH CENTURY
Martin Conway

For more information visit our web site

www.oup.co.uk/vsi

Andrew Ballantyne

ARCHITECTURE

A Very Short Introduction

To Di Leitch

OXFORD
UNIVERSITY PRESS

Great Clarendon Street, Oxford OX2 6DP

Oxford University Press is a department of the University of Oxford.
It furthers the University's objective of excellence in research, scholarship,
and education by publishing worldwide in

Oxford New York

Auckland Bangkok Buenos Aires Cape Town Chennai
Dar es Salaam Delhi Hong Kong Istanbul Karachi Kolkata
Kuala Lumpur Madrid Melbourne Mexico City Mumbai Nairobi
São Paulo Shanghai Taipei Tokyo Toronto

Oxford is a registered trade mark of Oxford University Press
in the UK and in certain other countries

Published in the United States
by Oxford University Press Inc., New York

First published as a Very Short Introduction 2002

British Library Cataloguing in Publication Data
Data available

Library of Congress Cataloging in Publication Data
Data available

ISBN 978-0-19-280179-1

9 10 8

Typeset by RefineCatch Ltd, Bungay, Suffolk
Printed in Great Britain by
Ashford Colour Press Ltd, Gosport, Hants.

Contents

List of illustrations

Introduction

I met a traveller from an antique land
Who said, 'Two vast and trunkless legs of stone
Stand in the desert. Near them, on the sand
Half-sunk, a shattered visage lies, whose frown
And wrinkled lip, and sneer of cold command,
Tell that its sculptor well those passions read
Which yet survive, stamped on these lifeless things,
The hand that mocked them, and the heart that fed;
And on the pedestal these words appear:
"My name is Ozymandias, King of Kings,
Look on my works, ye mighty, and despair!"
Nothing beside remains. Round the decay
Of that colossal wreck, boundless and bare,
The lone and level sands stretch far away.'

(Percy Bysshe Shelley, *Ozymandias*, 1818)

Buildings can be the most expensive things that civilizations produce. They can absorb any amount of effort and money if they are to compete with the great buildings of rivals, and of the past. It might seem misguided to try to outdo others when the costs are so high, but no one remembers the civilizations that took such a decision, at least not in architectural history. By contrast civilizations such as ancient Egypt and Rome, which built extravagantly, seem unavoidable. The imperishable buildings seem to go hand in hand with an imperishable reputation, which has always been the appeal of monuments for the powerful. When enough time has passed, all human achievements can seem fragile, and Shelley's famous poem *Ozymandias* shows both the attraction of the monumental and also how delusory its promise of everlasting glory can be. One of the things that matters about architecture is how it gives us clues to what really mattered to rulers of the past. Another thing is how it makes it possible for us, the living, to live in certain ways, and to demonstrate to each other and ourselves what it is that we really care about, as individuals and as a society. Different civilizations strike different balances between what seems to be owed to the living, and going beyond immediate needs in order to make things that build a reputation in posterity.

What this very short introduction tries to do is to explain how architecture goes about doing what it does. Buildings keep us warm and dry, and are closely involved in the practicalities of living, but 'architecture' always has a cultural dimension to it, if we choose to pay attention to it. Chapter 1 is about how buildings are involved with our sense of who we are. Chapter 2 looks at the way in which buildings are made to look like one another, so that they carry the right sort of messages to those 'in the know' in a particular culture. Chapter 3 considers what it is that makes some works of architecture come to be more culturally important than others.

One of the things that makes buildings particularly interesting to archaeologists is that they are caught up in so many aspects of life. The way they are organized tells us something about the way people interact in them, if we can work out which groups of people are brought together, and which kept apart. The materials from which buildings are made, and the way the materials are handled, can also tell us a great deal. If the stone came from a long way away, then we know that either there was an efficient transport system or that the stones were very special and worth a great deal of effort. If a building has a steel frame, then we know that it belongs to the modern age because the ancient world didn't know about them.

Buildings are an important part of the evidence available to us in knowing about what went on in the distant past, and they also tell us a good deal about what we really care about now. If we, as a society, allow motorways to be built across the countryside, then it can only happen because our care for the countryside is less than our desire to travel conveniently. As individuals we might have made a different decision, but as a society, given the flows and concentrations of money that circulate, and given the political processes that mediate the decisions, the buildings that surround us are produced. As individuals, most of us can do very little to shape the built environment in general. In some circumstances, though, concentrations of wealth and power have made it possible for individuals to command great changes. It was said of the Roman emperor Augustus that when he came to Rome it was built in brick, but when he left it was marble. And Ozymandias (Rameses II) evidently commissioned grand and extensive works. Buildings can be beautiful and inspiring, but if they are built (rather than just imagined) then they always have an economic and political aspect, as well as an aesthetic aspect. There are other aspects too, such as the technical side of things. Will it stand up? Will it keep the rain out? Can it be kept warm? Will it overheat? Can I use it as a place where I can live the life I want? Do I want to be the sort of person who lives in a place like this?

Given that a building has all these aspects, it is possible to write about architecture in ways that bring one or another of them to the fore. A history of building technology would be one possibility. This would be a story of progress, as more technically sophisticated ways of building superseded the more primitive ones. There would be significant advances, like the introduction of cement, and the arch, and a demonstration of the new types of building that these innovations made possible. What we lose sight of in this particular narrative is the fact that, at a given time, it is likely that few buildings will be technically advanced. Most buildings are just ordinary, and do not fall down or stop being useful the moment a technical advance has been made. Just as many people in Europe live in houses that were built a hundred years or more ago, so in ancient Rome the vaulted structures for which we now particularly remember the Romans were not the buildings that made up the fabric of most of the city, and in fact nearly all the famous Roman structures date from quite late in the history of the Roman Empire, so they were unknown to most Romans. Most significantly, they were unknown to the only Roman writer on architecture whose writings are known to us: Vitruvius. He lived too early.

It is possible to exclude technical matters, or relegate them to the background. Then the history of architecture can become a story about different styles of building. One set of shapes gradually transformed into another over the course of time. This type of history makes it sound as if there is in architectural forms a will to evolve and develop. Traditions grow up, and the architects keep trying out new possibilities, some of which are seen as improvements and are copied by others, before being improved upon in their turn. This approach can lead to a preoccupation with stylistic analysis that can lose sight of the fact that there is a practical rationale to building. It can also lead to the setting aside of the social and economic issues, which can be interesting, and which are sometimes certainly the most important aspects of a building. There is also the complicating fact that things look different from close at hand and from a distance. What looks to us like a gradual change across the course of centuries might well have been a much less even-tempered process at the time. It is always unusual for people to change their ways of doing things, and often what happens when a new idea takes over is that a generation of people grows old and inactive, while younger people inculcated with the new idea take up the tools. Whether the change looks gradual or abrupt may depend on how far we are from the event. Tragedy is farce in close-up.

There is a great deal of architecture around, from the recent and distant past around the world. It would be impossible to collect it all together and present it to a reader, especially in a very short introduction. It is necessary to be selective, and the particular buildings that one selects will very according to the story that has to be told. The aim of this book is to open up ways of thinking about architecture that show how rich the topic is, which might make it confusing at times. The following chapters discuss different themes, and I have introduced buildings in order to help make particular points in the argument. Therefore the illustrated buildings are not ordered chronologically. In order to help give an idea of the order in which things happened, there is a timeline at the back of the book. It will be noticed that there are more examples of recent architecture than from the distant past. This is for two reasons. One is that there simply are more buildings now standing that are of recent date. The other is that we tend to be more interested in things that are closer to us. If I look at a pyramid as a building that stands for a civilization that lasted for, say, 3,000 years, then I can feel that in the grand sweep of things the coverage is adequate. But if I were to take the same approach to the architecture of the last 3,000 years, then I would feel that the coverage had been ludicrously inadequate. It would sound facetious and satirical to summarize European architecture in a single monument. The medieval cathedrals would be the large monuments from the middle of the period in question, but I would worry about presenting them as the only things that really mattered.

Clearly the point of view of the writer is implicated in the selections that are to be made, and my selections are shaped by my immersion in and formation by Western culture. Other points of view are possible, have validity, and would generate different choices. This is not to say, though, that the ideas presented here have no more than a personal significance. They connect with a tradition that has gone through many transformations and developments, and the ones that are closest to us seem perhaps to be the most significant. Perhaps computers, televisions, and telephones have given us not only new ways of living, but also new ways of being human in a global system of networks. From another perspective, however, these recent developments might look like the continuation of a tendency that has been developing over the last 200 years, or the last 500.

General chronology

The language of architectural history includes words that designate different styles of architecture, and they are associated with different places and times. It has been convenient to divide up the history of human culture into broad periods. It is possible to quarrel with the appropriateness of these divisions, but they are now well established in our language, and they are necessary for finding one's bearings. We start with the ancient civilizations of Greece and Rome, which were admired for their literature, philosophy, and grandiose ruins. These civilizations were called 'classic', as a term of approbation. They were seen as the basis of authority and accomplishment in artistic matters, and so the products of those societies were in a general way called 'classical'. The Oxford English Dictionary gives a date of 1607 for an early use of the word in this way (referring to texts, rather than architecture). The other important classical age was the contemporary one, beginning at the Renaissance, the rebirth of classical learning that was also known as 'the revival of letters'. This gives us four periods in the history of the world, two enlightened ages and two dark ages. There was the primordial world to which ancient Egypt belonged, then the classical world of ancient Greece and Rome. Then, between the fall of Rome and the Renaissance there was a middle age with nothing particular to recommend it: the medieval period. And then came the Renaissance, the modern age, reason, and progress. While this is an over-simplification, it is a useful one for understanding why different types of architecture have their different reputations. The architecture of the classical age was admired and imitated. The architecture of the medieval period was taken less seriously. This has all changed since the terms were coined. We now know a good deal more about the Middle Ages, and would not want to write off the architecture so readily. Nevertheless the periodization remains in place. We still talk about the 'Middle Ages', even when we don't mean to suggest that they deserve to be neglected, and have forgotten what they were supposed to be in between.

If we look more widely then this division of time becomes problematic, because the cultural changes that they signify were not in fact changes in the history of the world, just changes in Western European culture as we have chosen to constitute it. Not only were Asia and the Americas going through completely independent developments, even Eastern Europe developed quite differently. Ancient Greece is certainly included in the Western tradition, because of the influence it had on the Roman ways of thinking about fine buildings. Properly it makes no sense to speak of 'medieval Greece', because despite the fact that the Byzantine Empire produced memorable and sophisticated buildings, there was no Renaissance. In a way the whole of Byzantine culture was a succession of renaissances, and the Greek emperors' sense of who they were was built on their links back to the ancient world. In 1453, just at the point when we might want to say that the Greek 'middle ages' came to an end, the capital Constantinople was overrun and the cultural change relocated the city, now called Istanbul, in a different tradition, where it became the capital of the Ottoman Empire. This caused the flight of Greek scholars to the west, and was one of the causes of the upsurge of knowledge of ancient texts that was so important in bringing about the Renaissance. So it is clear that the idea of the Middle Ages and a Renaissance is a fairly local tradition. There was no medieval period in America, because there had not been a classical civilization. There was no medieval period to the east of Europe because there was no reawakening of classical culture. It is worth noticing also that there is some doubt about whether, with the Renaissance, we are talking about a change in the art world or in a wider socio-economic world. In architectural history it is commonly agreed that the Renaissance began in 1420, when Brunelleschi started to build the dome of the cathedral at Florence. The dome not only surpassed the achievements of the Roman dome-builders, but Brunelleschi is supposed to have made careful studies of Roman ruins before embarking on the enterprise.

In art history the corresponding break is seen to be with the discovery of geometrical perspective, in Brunelleschi's circle. However there was another far-reaching change that had been making more gradual progress, and that was the breakdown of feudal power as the merchant traders amassed fortunes that were greater than those of the hereditary princes. The sense of the novelty of Brunelleschi's artistic enterprise was perhaps more because it was funded by new money than because it marked any radical break with the artistic achievements of his predecessors. I would not want to argue that the break away from feudalism and the invention of geometric perspective might have sprung from a common cause, which to me sounds too metaphysical. What does make sense to me is that the adoption of the new art by the people with new money made it seem all the more radical a departure. In our own day we see the great fortunes made from film, music, and computer businesses taking their place alongside the great inherited fortunes, and a different sense of style is associated with the way of life. The houses of the rich and famous often do not conform to the established canons of respectable taste, and may not be treated seriously by architectural historians now, but in the future, looking back, they will look as astonishing and unrepeatable as the houses of the 18th-century landed aristocracy. And strange as it may seem, we could find our own era represented in the architectural history books by these outlandish creations that seem utterly remote from our own experience of living now. Written up with one critical agenda the story might be called 'Late Capitalism and the Triumph of *Kitsch*'. From another, imbued with the values of the new age, the same buildings could be exhibited as evidence that 'Your Dreams Can Come True'.

What I am trying to do here is to give a sense of how different perspectives influence what it is that we see when we see buildings. They are involved in a complex way with an indefinite number of cultural and technical matters, and therefore they can have different levels of significance in different spheres. Moreover, when we try to pigeonhole them in categories, they have ways of escaping. We establish the categories, but then have to acknowledge that if we look closely they are not exact, and there are borderline cases. The more we know about a specific culture, the more statements about it sound like sweeping generalizations. What looks like a gradual evolution from a distance might have been a painful disillusionment for individuals, and on the contrary something that looks like a fault-line across Western culture might actually have been a fairly gentle process that was no more traumatic than a number of other changes. Nevertheless, we need some sort of framework if we are to understand anything about our orientation in the subject, and this is the framework that we have. It is just as well, though, to realize that it must not be expected to carry too heavy a load.

A closer look

Within each of the broad periods mentioned above, there is room for subdivision. For example, when the ancient world is understood in a very general way it can be quite adequate to call the architecture of Greece and Rome generically 'classical', but for a more detailed discussion this would not be helpful. The architecture of ancient Greece itself has a classical era, the 5th century BC, preceded by an archaic era, and followed by the Hellenistic era. Rome has its own archaic period, a Republican, and then an Imperial period. These divisions are taken from a mixture of artistic and political changes. The work from the archaic periods looks less accomplished and developed than the later work, but the Greek Hellenistic and the Roman Imperial phases are political eras, which had an effect on architecture, because the increased concentration of wealth in each of these periods meant that some buildings could be more lavish than ever before.

In the medieval period many different styles of architecture developed. Churches that tried to imitate Roman vaults and arches are now called 'Romanesque'. Later churches that used pointed arches and more decorative window tracery are called 'Gothic'.

Gothic is subdivided into different local styles. In England we find the Early English, Decorated, and Perpendicular styles. In France we find High Gothic, Flamboyant, and Rayonnant. The names of local styles are mostly derived from ideas that describe the effect of the architecture, or the shapes of tracery. 'Romanesque' also refers us back to the form of the building, which is reminiscent of those of Rome. In England and northern France, Romanesque architecture can be called 'Norman', after the dukes of Normandy who commissioned it, so this is a 'political' name for the same style. Similarly the name 'Gothic' is political, in that it refers to a body of people, the Goths, who laid waste to Rome. This does not tell us anything useful about the architecture, but it does tell us about how the architecture was seen at the time that the name was coined, in the 17th century, long after the cathedral-builders had stopped building in that manner.

Similarly, it no longer seems quite satisfactory for us to think of ourselves as living in the late days of the Renaissance. At some time, somewhere, it must have come to an end, but just when that happened is difficult to decide. The austere work of Brunelleschi and Alberti was followed by more decorative work by architects such as Bernini and Borromini, that overlaid rich ornament on a classical background, in a manner that we call Baroque and which reached its fullest development in 18th-century France and Germany (Figure 11). While this is certainly part of the same tradition, there is a different range of artistic intentions here, and so there is a different stylistic name. There was a reaction to these excesses, when the elaboration was, so to speak, stripped away and the classical order made clear again. This movement, known as Neoclassicism, was also nourished with new knowledge from archaeological investigations in Greece, which brought to light a better understanding of the architectural forms of the ancient Greek world, which had been officially revered, even when they were not really known.

By the end of the 18th century, then, there were rival versions of classicism in circulation, based on various understandings of Greek and Roman architecture, ranging from the fundamentalist simplicity of austere Doric temples, to the highly ornamental work of the Adam brothers. There was also a growing antiquarian interest in medieval architecture that developed into the very serious-minded architecture of the Gothic Revival of the mid-19th century (Figure 5) and various forays into exotic spectacle, such as the Brighton Pavilion (Figure 3). This eclecticism has flourished ever since, more visibly at some times than at others, marking the fact that the tastes of the classes that have money to spend on building were no longer unified. If the Renaissance marked the passing of power from the feudal to the mercantile classes, the coming of eclecticism marked the arrival of the great industrial fortunes. The people who made their money from the East India Company, from sugar plantations in the West Indies, or from industrial production in England, did not feel bound by the aristocratic canons of taste, and they experimented in idiosyncratic ways. There has been no consensus since, despite a concerted attempt to promote an internationally unified style for modern architecture through the CIAM (*Congrès internationaux d'architecture moderne*) guided by the Swiss architect Le Corbusier in the mid-20th century starting in 1928. He enthused about the poetic qualities of machines, ships, and grain silos, which were held up as models for the new architecture. While the architecture of the Modern Movement (also known as the International Style) dominated the architectural journals, it was rarely adopted by (for example) builders of housing aimed at a popular market, where versions of vernacular architecture, mock-Tudor, and notional Regency styles predominated. CIAM's consensus was maintained by excluding voices with alternative views about what modern architecture should be like, and it broke down altogether in 1959, since when contemporary architecture has been very varied (Figures 18, 19, 24, 25).

The terminology used to label the architecture of the last few decades has tended to shift its meaning as new buildings have appeared that

1. AT&T Building, New York (1978–80); architect: Philip Johnson (born 1906). Philip Johnson had been involved in a hugely successful exhibition 'The International Style', that introduced modernist architecture to the USA in 1932. He

worked with Mies van der Rohe on the authoritatively modern Seagram Building (Figure 18) and his writings had on the whole been persuasive in the modernist cause, though they made some mischief along the way. His design for the AT&T building, making use of classical motifs such as the broken pediment against the skyline, was seen as profoundly shocking at the time. It caused a furore and the architect was pictured on the cover of *Time* magazine. The building was correctly described as marking a turning point in attitudes to architecture, and in the following years there were many more colourful and flamboyant designs, which make the AT&T Building (now owned by Sony) look restrained and sober.

seem to need new labels. The term 'postmodern' was used to describe some of Le Corbusier's late buildings, such as the pilgrimage chapel at Ronchamp, which has pronounced sculptural qualities and had clearly moved on from the 'machine aesthetic' that he had previously been promoting. The term however did not catch on with a wide architectural public until later, when Charles Jencks published *The Language of Postmodern Architecture* (1977). He associated postmodernism with a concern for the meaning of buildings. However a less exact usage of the word is in circulation, as a name for the fashion for making use of noticeably historical forms in modern buildings, especially when they were used in ways that undermined their original effect, for example by being made of lightweight materials, being enlarged to gigantic size, or being brightly coloured. Commercial buildings of this type dating from the 1980s are to be seen in many cities around the world (Figure 1). There have been other rallying cries and manifestos in the architecture-world since then, but they have not as yet been given names that have made a lasting impression on a wide public. Frank Gehry's art museum in Bilbao might conceivably be presented as an example of Deconstructivism (Figure 24), but an explanation of what that term means certainly lies beyond the scope of a very short introduction to architecture.

The text that follows

In the chapters that follow, the text is organized in a fairly conversational way, moving between views of different aspects of the buildings that are used as examples. I have tried wherever possible to refer points back to the buildings that are illustrated, which may give an exaggerated impression of a building's importance, when it is used to make different points at different places in the text. The buildings are not discussed in the order that they were built, but they are all located on the timeline at the end of the book (p. 117). It will be noted that the buildings are not spread evenly across the time that is spanned, but are disproportionately from times close to our own.

In Chapter 2, the classical tradition is pieced together from a series of buildings beginning in the relatively recent past, and moving backwards in time, which may seem like a perverse way to order the material. In fact it reflects the way in which we piece together our traditions. We start with a familiar building (in this case Monticello, which is one of the most visited buildings in the world) and look for its precursors. Then we look for the precursors' precursors, and so on. Then what usually happens is that the sequence is reversed, to move forward in time, and that produces a narrative drive that brings with it an idea of forward movement, and it seems that the point of the whole tradition was to bring about the flowering of the final most developed works. This effect of historical narratives can be used in order to persuade us that one type of architecture is right for the future, or for the present. If we approach the present from a particular direction then it is obvious where the next step will take us. If we approach it from a different direction, then the next step will be going somewhere else. I have tried to avoid this kind of tendency in the text, but if I am asked what the architecture of the future will be like, then my answer is that it is likely to be more varied than ever before.

Since the end of the Middle Ages, commerce has been gaining

ground steadily. Productivity and efficiency have been increasingly important in everyday lives, especially with the development of the industrial revolution, and then telecommunications and the information revolution. Whatever the commodity, we expect it to be with us quicker than was possible a hundred years ago, or ten years ago. Whatever the task, we expect that it will be done more speedily and with less human effort. In order to make things more efficient, we divide up complex tasks into simple ones, and we all become more specialized. This causes fragmentation of knowledge. Our cultures tend to separate out, so that even the mass media, like television, now reach smaller more specialized audiences, because there are more stations than there used to be. It would be astonishing if, against this cultural background, architecture were to find a new consensus. The generality of architecture never conforms to the canons of taste of any particular 'high culture'. The traditions of high culture in architecture are pieced together from carefully selected buildings of the finest quality that remind us of what can be achieved by noble endeavour. It is comforting to think that we will not have to explain to an archaeologist from another age how it came to be that we were surrounded by buildings such as those that we actually have, and we turn a blind eye to most of them. Buildings always tell the truth, but in an ambiguous way, bearing many possible interpretations. In Manchester, a new shopping centre has great atrium spaces and classical columns with gilded capitals, looking the very image of excess, like a setting from the last days of Rome. I expect that architecture will connect with a variety of élite and popular traditions, and we will continue to find buildings that are close together on the ground that connect with cultures from disparate parts of the globe. The place where I have seen this tendency at its most marked is in Singapore, where I came across a Mongolian café next to an Italian–American pizzeria, with an Irish pub across the way. They were in a shopping and leisure complex that had been made by converting an old colonial building, the Convent of the Holy Infant Jesus, the chapel of which is still in use, especially for weddings, and is ablaze with the light from rows of sparkling chandeliers.

Chapter 1
Buildings have meaning

Home (and away)

Whenever we venture out into the world, we set out from home, and compare the unfamiliar things we meet with things that we already know. The home is charged with meaning, because it is the basis of what we know, and is closely involved with the most personal aspects of our lives. It has witnessed our indignities and embarrassments, as well as the face that we want to show the outside world. The home has seen us at our worst, and still shelters and protects us, so we feel secure there, and have surprisingly strong feelings for it, even though they go unnoticed most of the time. The same feeling can be invested in other things, and they too can contribute to the feeling of 'being at home'. Anything that we recognize as familiar, even something as immaterial as a tune, can somehow become ingrained, so that it becomes somehow a part of where we are, and if it is portable, like a tune, or a memorable episode in a novel, or an idea of how it is right to behave, then these things are part of who we are. We carry these immaterial things around with us, along with an idea of home. The building that we call home we leave in one place, and when we wander we wander away from it. A nomadic tribe, carrying its tents along with it, has an altogether different sense of what home is, but 'we' (those of us with a home that stays put) can feel at home in surroundings that are not actually our own, if they have familiar characteristics, whether or not they actually look like the places where we live. If I have a deeply ingrained expectation that I will hear a family or neighbours around me, making their own human noises as they go about their own lives, then I might find myself disturbed by the eerie silence to be found in an isolated house, or worried by the creaking of unfamiliar timbers, juddering of strange plumbing, hooting of owls, or scampering feet that I hear in the night. There are many aspects to the home, and the actual solid building is only a part of it. The thing that matters most about my home is that I know it, and I do not think about that most of the time, only really noticing it when something changes, such as when I move house, or when I have unfamiliar visitors and cannot behave with my usual levels of freedom. I have to acknowledge different (temporary) thresholds as I move about the house, if I don't want to walk in and surprise them. Business hotels try to make their rooms consistently the same, so that we start to feel at home in the whole hotel chain, not just in one building, even if we are in distant and unfamiliar parts of the world that we have never visited before. We know what to expect and more or less where we will find it, so we can continue with the minimum of disruption, and have contact with local character in controlled and limited doses, returning to a temporary substitute 'home' in the hotel. We can use our intuition, and it will work. Moving in an unfamiliar culture always turns up little moments of disorientation, such as when the disreputable-looking man in the bar claims that Margaret Thatcher is his mother as well as mine (which he seems to mean as a gesture of camaraderie) or a motor cycle screeches to a halt and I am asked, puzzled, why I'm not in a taxi – a question no one has ever asked me in Europe. These moments are stimulating, in their way, and turn out to be memorable, but they remind me that I'm a long way away from home and the things I know. It is no wonder that the best travel writers always turn out to have a taste for the surreal, which can be turned into humour, anxiety, or enchantment, but is always a state of mind to be passed through, and is never quite the state of serenity associated with being at home.

To set out on a journey is one of life's great pleasures, holding out as it does the prospect of making discoveries and finding fresh stimulation; and returning home is also a pleasure, but of a different order. We would feel more distress if we were unable to return home than if we had never managed to set out, because 'home' is such an important reference point, and if we are deprived of it then we have incalculable problems of disorientation, which do not end when we find a new shelter. Moving house involves vague but persistent feelings of things not being quite right, which are quite different from knowing that one is visiting a strange place and will return home tomorrow. It involves finding a new set of habits, and therefore becoming a slightly different person. The building is only part of the story. It is caught up in a variety of activities, both physical and mental, that influence how we feel about that particular place. Architecture involves this cultural aspect of buildings, which can range from something very personal and idiosyncratic to something that everyone seems to agree upon. We are shaped by the culture that we grow up in, and by the culture in which we participate, whether we think about it or not – and most of the time we don't think about it at all. In fact we are least aware of this at home. It is when we travel that we see that other people do things differently, and this can be disconcerting. In a western shopping mall we do not expect to be touched, but in a North African *souk* the shopkeepers sometimes reach out and tap your elbow or grasp your arm, to attract attention, which I found disconcerting. It upset my ingrained sense of what was proper, and because all the shopkeepers seemed to do it, it felt as if there was a conspiracy, compounded of course by the fact that they spoke to one another in a secret language that I didn't understand. This trivial paranoia is dispelled with a little knowledge and a little thought, but the ingrained instincts affect one's feelings before the rational thought does: I felt threatened, and knew that I shouldn't, but had to keep telling myself not to feel that way. The feeling wears off after a while, and if I had been brought up in the other culture, it would have been the self-evidently 'natural' way to behave, and I might have wondered when I visited a western shopping mall, why everyone was avoiding me: what did they think was wrong with me? In architecture, as in any other culture, our sense of 'how things should be' develops from our experience. Each gesture that we make means something, but the meaning depends on the culture in which the gesture is understood. Architecture is gesture made with buildings.

Cultures in the plural

A culture, in the sense that I mean here, need not involve a great many people. It might be vague and vast, as it would be if one were to want to contrast European culture with that of, say, Latin America; but equally, it might just involve a few people who have something in common and who therefore exchange glances and knowing smiles when, say, a teacher or an elderly relative says something that was not intended to be obscene, but is to those who hear the *double entendre* and absolutely must not laugh. Here there would be a single utterance, heard in two cultures of interpretation. In this sense we are involved with different cultures in different parts of our lives, when we deal with different groups of people. We are routinely accustomed to behaving in different ways in different settings, without particularly thinking about it. When the circumstances are familiar, we know how we expect ourselves to behave. We treat people we know well differently from strangers. We sit differently on public transport and on the sofa at home. We are comfortable saying some things to our friends, and a different range of things to our parents. We have a sense of decorum for our behaviour, and sense much the same with buildings. Some buildings seem to do the right thing, and we are comfortable with them, even if we don't pay them much attention. Others might seem awkward or wrong. For example there would be something wrong if a private house looked like a high street shop, and seemed to be trying to encourage people to come across the threshold to explore. The problem wouldn't just be the practical one, that people kept walking into the house, because that could be solved by keeping the door locked. The architectural problem is at a cultural level: the building would be making the wrong sort of gesture for a house.

One of the things that complicates architecture is that it can be significant to us in a variety of different ways. For example, the building I live in, which I think of as my home, carries a special feeling for me that it does not carry for people who don't live in it. I understand that and don't expect them to feel the same way as I do about my home, though I might expect them to feel about their home the way I do about mine (and sometimes I would be wrong, because in fact not everyone does feel the same). Other buildings seem especially beautiful, or spectacular in some way. If I am impressed with them, then I might expect that others will be similarly impressed (again, I might be wrong in individual instances, but I would feel that it was worth asking). And there are other buildings that are famous works of architecture that everybody knows are good. If I don't feel that a building of this sort is wonderful, then I might feel that I should keep quiet about the fact, because everyone seems to know for a fact that it is excellent, and if I don't agree then perhaps people will think that my judgement is faulty. These 'canonic' works are discussed in Chapter 3. Chapter 2 looks at the way in which buildings are made to look like one another, so that they carry the right sorts of messages to those 'in the know' in a particular culture. Chapter 1, this chapter, mainly looks at how buildings are involved with our sense of who we are.

Buildings are constructed so as to solve practical problems, but they often do more than that, and when they do then we feel inclined to call them 'architecture', because they have a cultural dimension. Of course any building at all can have a cultural dimension if we choose to pay attention to it, but often we feel disinclined to do that. For example, when I fill my car up with fuel, I don't necessarily think of the petrol station as 'architecture', just as a reasonably serviceable place. But I can start to think of it as architecture if I consider that petrol stations are culturally significant buildings, and that their design is worth looking at for what it can teach us about our attitudes to the car and the importance we attach to it.

Added value, cultural value

What architects do is to design buildings with an eye not only to their practical utility, but also with an eye to their cultural value, trying to give them a shape that is in some way appropriate. What it is that makes a building appropriate will be different in different circumstances, depending on what the surrounding buildings are like, what method of construction can be used, and what role a building plays. What seems right in the suburbs might be strange in a city centre. The same shape of building might be simple and direct if it is built in timber, but downright odd if cast in concrete. A building that makes a good swimming pool does not necessarily make a good library – even if it can be made to work, the building's appearance could feel misleading. The things that follow on from the different sets of decisions feel like forces pulling the building in different directions. If the building's materials are what most govern the building's shape then it will go one way, but if the primary concern is to make it the best possible image of its use, then it will go another. All these forces can act independently of one another, at the same time on the same building, so that taking care of one of them might disrupt one of the others. The issue is further complicated by the fact that some ways of doing things have a higher status than others. For example, take something smaller than a building, which is more often bought: furniture.

Furniture belongs in buildings, and can have the kinds of overtones that make it seem like small portable architectural works. Some architects design furniture. The things that we choose to have around us when we furnish our houses and apartments tell us something about the sort of people we are. Everybody knows this. Film-makers and novelists especially make use of the fact by telling us about the places their characters inhabit in order to let us know what kinds of people they are. The bleak interior described as the dwelling place of James Joyce's character in 'A Painful Case' acts as an indication of that character's habits of mind, which lead him to turn away from affection when – fleetingly – it is offered:

> The lofty walls of his uncarpeted room were free from pictures. He had himself bought every article of furniture in the room: a black iron bedstead, an iron wash-stand, four cane chairs, a clothes-rack, a coal-scuttle, a fender and irons, and a square table on which lay a double desk. A bookcase had been made in an alcove by means of shelves of white wood. The bed was clothed with white bedclothes and a black and scarlet rug covered the foot. A little hand-mirror hung above the wash-stand and during the day a white-shaded lamp stood as the sole ornament on the mantelpiece. The books on the white wooden shelves were arranged from below upwards according to bulk. (James Joyce, from 'A Painful Case', in *Dubliners*, first published in Great Britain 1914: London: Minerva, 1992, p. 93.)

In *Fight Club*, the nameless protagonist's total immersion in consumer society is demonstrated by the care with which he furnishes his apartment:

> Everything, including your set of hand-blown green glass dishes with the tiny bubbles and imperfections, little bits of sand, proof that they were crafted by the honest, simple, hard-working indigenous aboriginal peoples of wherever, well, these dishes all get blown out by the blast . . . .
>
> Something which was a bomb, a big bomb, had blasted my clever Njurunda coffee tables in the shape of a lime green yin and an orange yang that fit together to make a circle. Well they were splinters now.
>
> My Haparanda sofa group with the orange slip covers, design by Erika Pekkari, it was trash now.
>
> And I wasn't the only slave to my nesting instinct. The people I

> know who used to sit in the bathroom with pornography, now they sit in the bathroom with their IKEA furniture catalogue.
>
> We all have the same Johanneshov armchair in the Strinne green stripe pattern. Mine fell fifteen stories, burning, into a fountain.
>
> We all have the same Rislampa/Har paper lamps made from wire and environmentally friendly unbleached paper. Mine are confetti. . . .
>
> It took me my whole life to buy this stuff. (Chuck Palahniuk, *Fight Club*, New York: Norton, 1996, pp. 43–4.)

In David Fincher's film of the novel the point is driven home quickly and effectively by having the nameless character, played by Ed Norton, look round the apartment and, before our eyes, the furniture materializes, a piece at a time, complete with its catalogue description, so we can see that everything in the room has been valued, selected, and paid for. The point to be made here is that the furniture goes beyond being functional, and is described in each of these examples precisely because it does go beyond the functional. A chair in a film is never just a chair, it is an insight into character. Likewise, in a novel if a chair is described, it is always more than a place to sit. Of course the character has chairs in his apartment. If no mention were made of it then we would take it for granted. The character in *Fight Club* is morbidly self-aware, and asks himself a question that sane people do not ask themselves, but which advertisers and novelists ask of others all the time: 'What kind of dining set defines me as a person?' The question is not absurd, but it is not usually asked in this way of oneself. It sounds neurotic, certainly, but it isn't nonsensical. The sort of dining set that defines a president or an emperor is different from the mass-produced dining set that defines an insurance clerk as a person. But the questions that the insurance clerk would ask would normally tend to be either more practical or more vague: 'Will it fit in my apartment? Would I be happy to have this furniture around? Does it feel right?' If I am an emperor then the question is less concerned with a personal taste, and is more like: 'how do I demonstrate through my furniture that I'm no insurance clerk?' And the answer is: by having a table that is more extravagant than an insurance clerk could think of having. It may not work any better as a table, but in addition to working as a table it will impress and intimidate. One can imagine the chairman of a multinational company aspiring to own a table that had once belonged to Napoleon, and being prepared to spend a large sum of money on it if it became available. And one can imagine him thinking it money well spent.

Making gestures

Extravagance is not the only way to find gestural qualities in things, and enhance their status. An ascetic philosopher would aim for a table that was pointedly less extravagant than the norm, and its purpose would be to show high-mindedness rather than low status as such. A democratic president would need to show on different occasions both imperial grandeur (when entertaining visiting heads of state) and absolute ordinariness (showing a rapport with voters). We might feel ashamed if our head of state lived in an apartment with inexpensive catalogue furniture, but in another mood might resent the extravagant costs involved in furnishing high-status accommodation from the public purse. The architectural setting has a part to play in putting in place a sense of how it would be appropriate to behave, and in indicating the status and aspirations of its inhabitant. It can be simply a personal matter, if we don't care what anyone thinks, and decorate to suit ourselves, or can be very public theatre, broadcast around the whole world.

The meaning in buildings is not fixed in them. For example, the cottages that were built by agricultural workers for their own use were not considered as a form of artistic expression, but as serviceable shelters (Figure 2). However the romantic poets saw the simple cottages of the rural poor as an expression of tenacious

2. Traditional cottage, uncertain date, but pre-20th century; no architect. This hovel is a representative example of the types of dwelling that were built by the rural poor until the 19th century. Living conditions could be bad, but the worst cottages were made of earth and have long since disappeared. Stone dwellings, such as the one shown here, would have been built with stone that was either quarried locally or that had been cleared from the fields. This example would have been too small to adapt to modern needs, but many similar slightly larger buildings are still occupied, connected to electricity and with modern plumbing, which makes them very different from the places they once were. In Britain, most cottages are now inhabited by people whose income does not come from farming the plot of land on which the house sits, but by people who either have jobs in towns, or who have retired from their town work. Most cottages therefore function as part of a city, even though they can still look idyllically rural.

virtue in bleak circumstances, which meant that they were seen as gestural, and then by the end of the 18th century there was a fashion for small-scale rural retreats (*cottages ornées*), which certainly should be seen as artistically expressive, and were designed that way. There has been a long tradition of looking at agricultural workers as virtuous and romantic that started somewhere in the ancient world. It was already a tradition when Virgil wrote his *Eclogues* in the first century BC. Already then there was a sentimental interpretation of agriculture that could develop because there was a class in that society that did not have an everyday involvement in agriculture, but who could see it from a distance and think of it as enviable, or innocent. The most famous architectural expression of this sensibility in the 'modern' world is the hamlet that Marie-Antoinette commissioned at Versailles, where she could step aside from her duties as the queen in the world's most splendid court, and pretend to be a simple milkmaid, in touch with nature and her feelings. The gesture is a blend of innocence, naïveté and sauciness. Another example is Blaise Hamlet near Bristol, that was designed by the architect John Nash as a self-consciously pretty and well-managed group of houses for retired employees of the Blaise estate, a genuine but highly visible gesture of benevolence on the part of the landowner. This has particular poignancy because Nash was also responsible for one of the most extravagant princely dwellings of this or any other time: the Royal Pavilion at Brighton (Figure 3). Even in small illustrations, there is no doubt about the relative status of the inhabitants of the dwellings shown in Figures 2 and 3. Without any specialized knowledge of architecture, we know how to read the signs. Even if we thought that the building in Brighton was relatively normal, it would be clear that it was not the low-cost option, and in fact it was stylistically outlandish and novel. It was not only extravagant, it also relished the display of that extravagance, and still today sweeps visitors along with the sheer exuberance of its display. There is something charming about the way it refuses to acknowledge conventional decorum, and something absolutely apt about the way the Prince Regent's riotous

3. Royal Pavilion, Brighton, England (1815–21); architect: John Nash (1752–1835). This is one of the most self-consciously exotic buildings that has ever been built. The 'pavilion' at Brighton began with a much smaller and more conventional building for the then Prince of Wales (who was later Prince Regent and then George IV). The name 'pavilion' derives an old French word for a tent and is now normally used for small buildings that connect with outdoor activity, and it would have fitted the original building reasonably well, but the sprawling palace that developed on the site is not really a pavilion (though some of the roofs have tent-like forms). John Nash also designed the original Regent Street in London, and Buckingham Palace (but not its familiar public façade). The Pavilion was composed of architectural motifs taken from the far reaches of empire, with Indian domes and verandahs on the outside, and a sumptuous western idea of Chinese decoration on the inside.

parties would do the same. There is a surprisingly close relation between the form of the building and its function.

Extravagance is also the main reason to be impressed by the great pyramids of ancient Egypt. Vast resources went into making them, and from that we infer how powerful were the rulers who commissioned them. There are reasons to be impressed by the ingenuity of the pyramid builders, and their know-how, but the pyramids would be insignificant monuments, known only to specialists, if they were not big (Figure 4). We are not overly impressed by things that we think we could do ourselves, and the reason that the pyramids were one of the wonders of the world is that they could not easily be imitated, on account of the sheer expense of the undertaking. If the production of the state only just covered the people's need to subsist, then it would not have been possible to build on such a scale. And if the wealth had been evenly distributed through the society, then no such monument could have been built. A high proportion of the state's wealth must have been directed into these building programmes, and such a unity of will suggests a political structure that put a great deal of power at the disposal of an individual. The pyramids were given over to survival and prosperity in the afterlife, and so could be seen as a whole society's investment in the future. The Brighton Pavilion was given over to pleasure. What links the two buildings is that they are far from ordinary, and have little connection with the daily lives of the ordinary people in either society. Neither of them ever helped directly with the activities that make it possible to live, such as the production of food or the manufacture of useful goods. Those activities must have been going on somewhere in each society, but they are not housed in these buildings, which consumed vast resources. They impress because they bear the mark of that consumption – of materials carefully worked, to make effects that were carefully considered.

'Architecture' has often been taken to be impressive buildings such as these. In that way of thinking, buildings that impress us are to be

4. Great Pyramid of Khufu, Giza, near Cairo, Egypt (2723–2563 BC); architect: unknown. The Egyptian pyramids astonished the ancient world, and in the modern world have been a byword for mystery. They were built in the north of Egypt as burial places for the pharaohs – the god-kings who ruled in ancient times. The one illustrated here was the largest of them, built for the burial of Khufu, who is also known by the Greeks' name for him: Cheops. All the large pyramids date from the Old Kingdom of Egypt, after which the country was ruled from Thebes, 500 miles further south, and the burials were in cave tombs in the Valley of the Kings. The Great Pyramid is huge, and consumed vast amounts of effort from the society that built it – without the help of such advanced technology as iron tools or pulleys of any kind. Everyday buildings were built in mud-brick and timber, and they do not survive, but the pyramids were designed to last forever.

called 'architecture', while those that don't impress remain as mere 'buildings'. In fact we might not need to call them anything at all, because they probably just fall out of the picture. I want to argue that 'architecture' is not the same thing as 'good buildings' but is the cultural aspect of any building at all, good or bad. The putting together of materials belongs to the realm of building, but the building's gestures – the extravagance, exoticism, and exuberance – belong to the realm of architecture, as would simplicity and ruggedness, if those were the building's particular qualities. The point is best explained by thinking about 'vernacular architecture', which is the term used to refer to the ordinary buildings put up by ordinary people, traditionally agricultural workers building for themselves or their neighbours. If we were to look at these buildings through the eyes of an 18th-century landowner, then we would see them as 'hovels', places to live that had few comforts – though for the people who lived in them they would have had all the complicated connotations of 'home'. When we as tourists in the Lake District see them they are 'vernacular architecture' and a charming part of the scenery, protected by legislation. Even when the actual fabric of the building has not changed much, there has been a change in sensibility, which can be traced back to the influence of the Romantic poets, especially Wordsworth. The point to be made is that 'architecture' did not seem to be anything to do with these buildings when they were built, but it does seem to be there now. The stones have not moved. It is the culture that has shifted. Architecture is not an attribute of a building in itself, but of a building that is experienced in a culture – and we all bring some culture or other to bear on a building when we experience it. This is not to say that all buildings are equally good, or important, only to say that every building has its cultural aspect, and if we choose to notice it then we are looking at that building as architecture. Without some cultural intuitions we would not be able to sense any significant difference between the peasants eating round the fire in a little cottage, and the nobility and revellers eating in the dining room of the Brighton Pavilion – more food, more noise, more people. The peasants may not have taken a self-conscious decision about what kind of dining set defined them as people, but nevertheless the way they dined, or rather supped, speaks volumes about them and their way of life. The architecture is caught up in a way of life, and we make inferences about the life from interpreting the architecture. Conversely we either deliberately choose to live in surroundings that reflect our ideas about who we are, or else find ourselves living in conditions that somehow reveal more about us than we realize.

Local landmarks

One of the things that makes our surroundings feel right is familiarity. We grow accustomed to our surroundings and shape our habits around them, so that even if the surroundings interfere with what we're trying to do, we are accustomed to dealing with the problems. Buildings which are part of the daily scene come to have significance simply by being there. It is possible for a building with no artistic accomplishment to become meaningful and significant for large numbers of people, simply by having been there all their lives. In the same way that I feel at home in my house, I feel a bond of recognition when I see a familiar landmark, and some buildings have been designed with that role in mind. For example the very prominent city hall in Philadelphia has this role for the inhabitants of the city. Artistically it is quite an odd building, and it has not been widely imitated by architects in other parts of the world. Its principal significance is local, but locally it is very significant indeed. For many years it was the tallest building in the city – a statue of the city's founder, William Penn, stands at the top of its tower, and it was seen as symbolically appropriate that he should not be overtopped. The city centre's streets are planned on a grid, which is broken by the city hall, so it is the one building in the centre that stops vistas, and it is visible from a long way off. The oddity of the design makes it unique and identifiable with this single point on the surface of the earth. It is not a generic interchangeable building that could be anywhere and just happens to be here, but is a symbolic anchor-point around which the city grew. The city hall therefore acts as a symbol of the status of the city and the state of Pennsylvania.

National monuments

At national level something similar happens, but at a larger scale. The buildings that represent the nation to itself are grander again, and more generally recognized, because they also have a role in representing the nation to the rest of the world. In Washington DC, the Capitol building, the White House and the monuments along the Mall have become the buildings that have this symbolic role, and they have a duty to reflect the status of the nation on the international stage. In the UK the equivalent monuments are the Houses of Parliament (the Palace of Westminster), Buckingham Palace, and the ministries along Whitehall, running up into Trafalgar Square. In Paris there is a significant difference, because the monuments that have the greatest symbolic prominence are not seats of government, but of culture. The Champs Elysées from the Louvre to the Arc de Triomphe, and the Eiffel Tower have come to represent the identity of the French nation overseas more evocatively than the National Assembly and the president's palace. Where the capital city did not already provide the necessary accretion of monuments, some nations have erected a purpose-designed national monument, such as in Budapest, where an architectural composition supports a weight of symbolism from various sources – Christian, pagan neoclassical, and historical – to show that the Hungarians are descended from wild horsemen, but are now part of the civilized colloquy of nations. The various states in Italy did not unify into an Italian nation until the 19th century, and the vast Victor Emmanuel monument in Rome was designed to commemorate the event, and remind all Italians of their new collective identity, drawing on the Roman imperial past. These monuments are in the capital cities of various nations, but their role is to act as a symbol for people who live beyond the city.

A building such as the Palace of Westminster has a double role to play. It must work reasonably well as a building in which to do parliamentary business, and it must also appropriately symbolize the collective identity of the nation's policy-makers. We are routinely familiar with the symbolic role, and have no difficulty in recognizing the building as one of the 'sights' of London (Figure 5) but are less familiar with its internal organization, which is complex but highly rational – if seen with reference to the activities that were anticipated when it was built. Much has changed since then, and the building has not helped that change, but it was planned round a central axis, with the House of Lords on one side, the House of Commons on the other, and an imposing vaulted lobby in between. A tremendously long corridor runs along the line of the river frontage, leading to a sequence of committee rooms. The rooms were all daylit, and naturally ventilated, because when they were built there was no viable alternative, and in order to make that possible there are courtyards and lightwells. The rationality of the planning affects how well the building works as the parliamentarians go about their business, but has nothing to do with the building's symbolism, which evokes the medieval past, as a way of demonstrating continuity with that past. This was not intended to be seen as a 'revolutionary' building. The building replaced an earlier parliament building, which had been medieval, but there were more reasons than inertia for rebuilding in a medieval style. The Gothic style developed in the Christian cathedrals of northern Europe, so it was seen as more indigenous than the most obvious alternative, which would have been some form of classicism, which has its roots in pagan Greece, and was first imported to Britain by Roman invaders. The architecture here was intended to help along an idea of British identity that was deeply rooted in the place, and rather pious, and because we still recognize many of the architectural gestures, the symbolism still seems to work, even though there have been many social and cultural changes since the building was constructed.

It is not inevitable that a building with a national role would have to appeal to the country's sense of its ancient identity. When Scotland

5. Palace of Westminster, London, England (1836–68); architect: Sir Charles Barry (1795–1860) with A. W. N. Pugin (1812–52). The old Palace of Westminster, where the British parliament met, was burnt down in 1834. It was replaced by the present building, the organization of which was worked out by Sir Charles Barry, while Augustus Pugin designed the medieval-style decoration, not only of the outside of the building, but also of the furniture and the wallpaper. Views of the outside are very familiar: the romantic silhouette and walls covered in panels of intricate but mechanically repetitive carving. The design was chosen in competition, and it stipulated that the design had to be medieval in character – taking inspiration from the surviving parts of the old palace, such as Westminster Hall. Barry enlisted Pugin's help because Pugin was passionate about medieval architecture, which he described as an indigenous Christian architecture, in contrast with the pagan origins of classicism.

6. Chandigarh, Punjab, India (1950–65); architect: Le Corbusier (1887–1965). Le Corbusier drew up a masterplan for the new administrative capital, and designed its principal administrative buildings: the Secretariat, the High Court, and the Assembly. There were particular climatic problems to be addressed, and the architecture is dominated by shading devices, such as an umbrella-like roof over the top of the whole of the High Court building. Surrounding the buildings as far as possible with shade, it was also necessary to promote the circulation of air. A river was dammed in order to make a lake that helped to modify the local climate. The buildings are composed of Le Corbusier's usual interplay between grid-like forms, and freely sculptural elements, made out of concrete by a local workforce.

needed a new building to house its national assembly, it chose Enric Miralles, an avant-gardist architect from Barcelona. The choice was calculated to show that Scotland is not provincial, but has a presence on the world stage, and that it is forward-looking. There was a similar concern to position the Punjab in the modern world when Le Corbusier was given his largest commission, to design a capital city, Chandigarh (Figure 6). In this respect the commission was a great international success. By this time in his career, Le Corbusier had had a tremendous influence on how people thought about how to make cities work. His most famous image of urban design was a model that showed Paris with its boulevards flattened, making room for a grid of enormous residential tower blocks. Needless to say, the idea was not acted on. The ideas had more immediate impact in Latin America, where there were rapidly growing cities and centralized power structures that could see them implemented, but they were designed by others, not the originator of the thinking. Chandigarh was the only city designed by Le Corbusier that was actually built, so it was much anticipated around the world. It presented the architect with particular challenges, in finding ways to make an impression on the sophisticated international architecture scene, while having at his disposal only the materials and craftsmanship to be found locally, and which make it in its way profoundly rooted to the place.

Ancient Egypt in the modern world

It does not always happen that the symbolism designed into a building is the symbolism that is understood by the observer who sees the building in the modern age, and the more distant the culture the more likely it is. For example, the pyramids have been seen as a symbol of ancient mystery, not because that was any part of the intention of their designers, but because they were so remote from modern rationalism, and so little understood. Voltaire poured scorn on the ancient Egyptians' reverence for cats and onions. The air of mystery was deliberately exploited when pyramids were evoked in Western culture, and the 'Egyptian' rites in freemasonry were devised in the 18th century. One major advance in our appreciation of ancient Egypt was made in the 19th century when hieroglyphics, ancient Egyptian writing, were deciphered for the first time. The archaeological study of Egypt has advanced enormously, and some aspects of the society are now understood quite clearly. In a society that lasted for hundreds of years at a stretch without noticeable cultural change, the habits of the culture (however bizarre they might seem to us) would surely have been experienced as the most obvious sort of common sense by the people who lived then. *Of course* priests dress up in costumes to look like the gods: that's what priests do. *Obviously* some sacred ceremonies are performed at dead of night – that's the proper time for them. But in our own day the popular imagination continues to develop the old idea of supernatural powers, curses, and occult knowledge, often linking it with futuristic technical wizardry. The basic 'argument' is that, since the achievements of the ancient Egyptians were so impressive, they must have had help from advanced technologies, like laser beams, or visiting spacecraft, and from there it is a small step to think that they might have discovered how to bring the dead back to life. This imaginative tradition is sold as fact in some of the literature (which outsells academic studies by a factor of tens or hundreds of thousands) and in an overtly fictional way is to be found in such films as *Raiders of the Lost Ark*, *The Mummy*, *Stargate*, and *The Fifth Element*. The imagery is evidently effective in its appeal to modern audiences, and the fact that the ancient Egyptians would not recognize themselves or any of their ideas in the stories is not an issue. At least, it isn't an issue unless we have misinformed ourselves to the point that we think that we're watching these films in order to find out about ancient Egypt. And that would be a straightforward but terrible error. The films tell us about the daydreams of the present day, not about the ancient past. The buildings of the pharaohs were certainly intended to have meaning. It is evident from the care and precision with which they were worked. They are not the products of neglect and chance. But equally we can be sure that the original meaning is lost to us today, and attempts to reconstruct it can only be conjecture and will never have the force of immediate intuition. The original architects might have felt that they were building things that had definite meaning embodied in them, but with the passage of time and the perishing of civilizations, it becomes clear that the meaning is volatile, and dependent not just on the stones, but also on the culture in which the interpretation is made.

Classical and Gothic

The buildings that are most consistently associated with virtue and high-mindedness in the Western tradition are the buildings of ancient Greece, especially the Parthenon in Athens, which has always been seen as a high point of artistic accomplishment (Figure 7). One of the things that marks out Athens culturally is that a great many ideas were developed there that are with us still – ideas such as democracy, and philosophy. The monuments that were built at the time of the golden age of Athens, in the 5th century BC, are associated with the foundations of Western society, and because of that association have unmatched authority. This was the case even during periods of time when the actual form of the buildings was not widely known, such as in the 18th century, when the ancient sanctuary was used for military purposes by the Turks – and casual visitors have never been welcomed into military bases. Also by then the form of the ancient buildings was not altogether clear, because there had been an accumulation of various additions – towers and fortifications. Back in ancient times, classical architecture had been adopted by the Romans, and their versions of it spread throughout their vast empire – across Europe, and into Africa and the Middle East. There have been many versions of this 'classical' architecture over the centuries, and it has been understood in different ways, so we find it adopted for its democratic and philosophical overtones by Thomas Jefferson when he laid out the university campus at Virginia, inspired by the ideals that launched the constitution of the newly independent USA, while Albert Speer played up its capacity for imperial pomp in his designs for Hitler's Berlin. There was a vogue for specifically Greek classicism among Irish Catholics in the

7. The Parthenon, Athens, Greece (447–436 BC); architects: Ictinus and Callicrates working with the sculptor Phidias. The Parthenon was the largest of the Greek temples from the 5th century BC, the 'classical' age of Greece. It was extravagant, on account of decorations and refinements that are not apparent in a general photograph. Phidias, the greatest sculptor of the age was employed here, certainly to make the cult figure of the goddess Athena, and perhaps to supervise the building works. There were fine sculpted decorations showing Greeks wrestling with centaurs and Amazons in the square panels visible above the columns that run right round the building. Uniquely there was also a frieze in low relief on the wall of the temple, depicting a great procession. The building is of solid marble, which can be worked very precisely, and the use of optical refinement is more evident here than anywhere else. All the architectural lines that look straight are in fact very slightly curved.

earlier 19th century, because they felt kinship not with the ancient but with the modern Greeks in their struggle for independence.

The use of classical columns and decorative detail has been so regularly revived in the history of Western architecture that they more or less define what Western architecture is, or was seen to be, until relatively recently. Even the main alternative tradition – the medieval architecture that we now call Gothic – grew out of an attempt to rival the Romans' achievements in their monuments. The vaulted churches of northern Europe that were built from the 10th to the 12th century are called 'Romanesque', and they were inspired by the ruins of Roman gates and temples that lingered for example in Burgundy, where we find the first medieval vaulted church at Tournus. The meaning of medieval buildings has undergone the most extraordinary shift over the years. The most spectacular monuments of the Middle Ages are the great French cathedrals, such as Bourges, which were made so as to appear as if they were constructed out of little more than coloured light (Figure 8). Complex and ingenious arrangements of stone made all this possible, cut to shape with astonishing precision, and put into place by groups of skilled craftsmen who would travel round from one major cathedral to another, learning from their experience and improving on past performances. While the various elements of the Gothic style were around in Romanesque churches, it is usually seen to have crystallized in a new vision in the fabulously wealthy church of Saint-Denis near Paris, from about 1137, when the Abbot Suger began a programme of rebuilding. He described his rapture, surrounded by the church's gem-encrusted treasures and coloured light: 'I see myself dwelling, as it were, in some strange region of the universe which neither exists in the slime of the earth nor entirely in the purity of Heaven.' Through the 13th to 15th centuries there were also pale imitations of the work in the smaller churches and more modest buildings.

The name 'Gothic' was first given to this architecture in the 17th century, as a term of abuse. The Goths, along with the Vandals and

8. Cathedral of St Etienne, Bourges, France (begun 1190). Of all the medieval cathedrals, this is the one that best illustrates the idea of a building as a cage of light. The west end of the building is immensely solid, with five unequal doorways surrounded by hundreds of small sculpted figures. Above there are two unequal towers. The rest of the building however gives an impression of being precisely repetitive, as a standard type of bay is taken along the whole length of the building without interruption, and adapted with a minimum of difference so as to make it turn the semi-circular end at the west. The nave is immensely high, at 39 m (125 feet), and it is flanked by double aisles. The building is filled with light that filters through stained glass, painted with images of biblical stories. From the outside the buttressing that holds the building up is clearly visible, looking like a series of powerful props: they shore up the illusion of weightless delicacy within.

Huns, were the Germanic tribes who sacked Rome and laid waste to the western Roman empire in the 5th century. To call the architecture 'Gothic' is like calling it 'barbaric' – saying that it is a form of cultural vandalism. Needless to say, in this cultural climate the architecture was not approached with sympathy, and it was not closely analysed, but all non-classical styles of building were bundled together and thought of as a confused jumble of incoherence and bad taste. This sense of the Gothic survives when it is used in 'Gothic horror'. Indeed the whole idea of the Middle Ages is caught up in this way of looking at things. It was supposed to have been a time between ancient and modern civilization (see page 6). Medieval architecture was studied first of all by antiquaries, who began to realize that there were various different styles of architecture here, and that they had been built at different times. The Gothic was then used in the 19th century by architects such as Pugin, who did the detailed work for the Palace of Westminster, but he preferred to call the style 'pointed or Christian' rather than Gothic, in an attempt to clear it of its unfavourable associations. For him, and architects like him, it came to represent a way of designing that was highly principled, and went well beyond being a pleasant decorative style, to being a moral and religious way of doing the right thing in architecture. For him Gothic architecture was not only the best, it was the only legitimate sort of architecture for a principled designer with Christian morals.

Architectural merit

One might want to ask, 'what is the real meaning of Gothic?' but the question doesn't allow a single answer that will satisfy everyone. If I react in a certain way to a building when I encounter it, then so far as I am concerned my reaction is genuine, and the way I react will depend on my previous experience. If it is the first time I have entered a Gothic cathedral, say, then I might be puzzled or impressed, seeing it as a place of wonder and mystery. If I have been in many other similar cathedrals then it might feel quite familiar, and I could find it steady and reassuring. I do not necessarily know what the designer intended me to feel. That does not mean that the experience must be without meaning for me. It is worth labouring the point, because architects tend to think of the matter differently. If an architect thinks of the design of buildings as a creative activity, then it is most likely that it would seem most important to work with sincerity and conviction, and less important to act with a view to second-guessing the reaction of an audience. Indeed, working with an eye on the crowd's response might seem to indicate a lack of authenticity. Buildings designed by this sort of architect will be the way they are because that is how the architect feels they must be, and any compromise with the views of others will be a weakening and worsening of the design. It tends to be the case that this is the sort of architect admired by other architects. To people who do not share the vision, the view may look arrogant and inflexible, but to people who do share it the architect will seem inspired. Conversely, an architect who is sensitive to the audience's response might take fewer risks, might tend to take a conservative view of cultural change, and might be seen as a reliable performer by the people who commission buildings, but such a designer will accrue no artistic *kudos*. Architects of this type greatly outnumber the others, but we do not hear about them in books about architecture, because, despite providing what society on the whole wants of them, they are seen by other architects at best as honest and competent but not particularly notable, or as slick commercial operators. Unqualified admiration is reserved for those who seem to manage to make their own ideas into buildings, and to bend the will of others to their own in order to make it happen. Indeed, this is no mean feat, because the will of the person paying for the building is usually the one that has most power, and so one of the great practical skills that architects need to have is the power to persuade.

Buildings, as I have said, are often very expensive. The person or committee that commissions a building will always want to be assured that its money is being spent wisely, in order to bring about what is intended. If a school commissions a swimming pool then it will be disappointed, and will undoubtedly sue, if the building that results from the commission cannot in fact be used as for swimming. If a plutocrat commissions a frivolous eye-catcher for a hill in his garden, then the architect will have failed if the building is solemnly monumental. How does the architect persuade the client that the design fits the bill? Usually by explaining what it is going to be like, by using illustrations or models, so that the building can be imagined in its setting. At this stage the design can be modified without great expenditure. The main alternative is to build the design, and modify the building if needs be, but to do this is for most of us ruinously extravagant. It is what Ludwig II of Bavaria did at his small and highly ornamental palace, Linderhof, in the foothills of the Alps, but his name has never been a byword for prudence, and his accountants eventually had him certified as insane. Often a building cannot be the way we would like it to be, perhaps because our neighbours will not allow it, or perhaps for some more fundamental reason, such as the limited strength of materials or the intransigent way in which gravity lets us down. In persuading the client that the building is as closely suitable for its purpose as can reasonably be expected, the architect has three main techniques of persuasion.

Reason

The first is reasoned argument. A design cannot develop solely by way of reasoning – there is always at some point a creative leap in the process, except perhaps in a very traditional society when we might decide that now is the moment to have a house like every other house we know. Even then, the appeal isn't really to reasoning as to the repetition of experience. Reasoning, in the strict sense of moving from agreed premises to necessary conclusions, is never the only way of thinking involved in finding a design, but it is necessary if one is to assess the merits of a given design. It should be possible to frame an argument that shows why a design is good, and this will amount to a demonstration that the design will do what it is supposed to do. In buildings where technical matters predominate, this might well be the main form of persuasion used in winning

9. Schröder house, Utrecht, Netherlands (1924); architect: Gerrit Rietveld (1888–1964). This small house was on the edge of Utrecht when it was built, on the end of a terrace of more conventional houses, looking out across the absolutely flat surrounding countryside. It was built for Mrs Schröder, a widow with children, who commissioned Rietveld, a furniture designer, to make a design that suited her ideas about how to live. On the upper floor an arrangement of folding and sliding screen walls made it possible to have a large open space, or to screen areas off to give individuals visual privacy – the screens did not allow much acoustic privacy. Rietveld was involved with the De Stijl group of artists, and the design of the house connects with their ideas about form, rather than with any traditional ideas about architecture or building. The appearance of the house was always extraordinary and novel, but its means of construction were fairly traditional, the walls being built of brickwork, rendered and painted.

approval for the design. However buildings are often complex, and have many factors working on them that interfere with one another. For example if I make some windows larger in order to let in more light or open up a view, then the building might let out more heat, and it could be necessary to install a more powerful heater. This actually happened at the house that Gerrit Rietveld designed for Mrs Schröder in Utrecht (Figure 9). The central heating system here was normally used for heating industrial space. It cost as much as a typical Utrecht house of the day, and made the cost of the whole house about twice that of an ordinary house of its size. The decision to install the heater must have been the result of reasoning, because it has no other obvious appeal. Given the novel form of the house, its unusual degree of openness to the outside, and the consequent loss of heat, the decision to install the heater was undoubtedly rational. However it is equally clear that the overall form of the building was not devised by way of reason alone – otherwise one might have decided on smaller windows and have had a house that was less costly both to build and to run.

Conviction

The house has had tremendous influence in the decades since it was built, and among architects it is one of the best remembered buildings of the 1920s, despite its small size and inconspicuous location – outside the town centre of a provincial town in a small country. If it had been known that it would keep the Schröder name imperishably in the public eye, then that might have been a reason for building a house in this way, but of course the house's reputation could not be predicted in advance, and this form of argument could not have been rationally allowed at the time that Mrs Schröder took the decision to build. What is more likely to have persuaded her of the rightness of the design was the force of Rietveld's personal conviction. The client had strong convictions of her own, about the way that life should be lived. Every bedroom could work as a small living room, and all the rooms could be thrown together into one big space by folding away the walls, which were just thin screens.

When the rooms were enclosed, each one had a door to the outside, and a wash basin in it. This was not just an ordinary house that the designer managed to make artistically adventurous – it was designed to accommodate a fresh way of living. Nevertheless, the reason that the house looked the way it did was because of Rietveld's involvement with the De Stijl group of artists (which included the painter Mondrian in its number) and he came to the project with experience in furniture design, following the principles of using lines and planes at right angles to one another, and primary colours. These might seem like odd principles to have adopted, but he did adopt them. His reasons for doing so need not detain us here, but involved a belief that by these means one could directly influence the state of the soul. It is quite possible that Mrs Schröder shared these convictions too, in which case she would have been persuaded by reason. If however she did not accept Rietveld's premises but was impressed by his seriousness of purpose and believed that he would achieve something worthwhile, then she would have been persuaded in a way that is used more often than it is acknowledged. In effect this is the same as convincing someone of one's authority to deal with the matter in hand, and it takes the general form of saying 'trust me, I am able to judge this better than you are'.

Seduction

The third form of persuasion is different again, because it does not claim authority, but rather charms the client into suspending criticism. This might be because the design is very appealing, or it might be because the architect is very appealing. It is not unknown for architects literally to seduce their clients, or their clients' wives. Frank Lloyd Wright eloped with the wife of one of his clients, and consequently had to abandon not only his family, but also his successful architectural practice. He was not the only one. Indeed Rietveld grew very close to Mrs Schröder, and set up a studio in the built-in garage of her house, and displayed his furniture designs there. The charmer in effect says 'indulge me, this is what I want, and you will love it because it is my work'. The power of both authority and charm come from either instructing or more gently persuading someone to stop reasoning, and accept advice. Individuals are more susceptible than are committees, and buildings commissioned by committees are correspondingly less idiosyncratic, more reasonable. A housing committee would never have commissioned the Schröder house. A committee formed to promote the ideals of De Stijl might have done.

A multiplicity of meanings

This little house neatly illustrates a variety of ways in which a building can have meaning. For the children who grew up in it, extraordinary though it may have been, it was home, and would have been a comforting and reassuring place to return to after a day at school. For the widow Schröder it was a basis for a fresh start and a new way of life after the death of her still young husband. For Rietveld it was an opportunity to put into practice on an unprecedented scale the ideas that he had been working on with his artist friends, and he did what it was necessary to do. For the neighbours the building must have seemed odd and unaccountable, and would have made no sense at all at first, but it gradually became familiar to them as a landmark at the edge of the town, looking out (as it did then) over flat open fields. In the 21st century the house looks 'ahead of its time', whatever that might mean, and if we were to think that we could guess at its date by looking at its style, then we would certainly guess some time after 1924, and might admire it for its apparent prescience. On the other hand we might look at its level of consumption of fuel and feel the need to condemn it on environmental grounds. There is one small building here, but many different ways to respond to it, so different sets of feelings are generated by it. Since architecture is what happens when we encounter a building and bring a culture to bear on it, we could say that this one building belongs to, or produces, a number of architectures. It makes a gesture in more than one cultural context. If we look at it as a work of architecture of the home, then it is a gesture of freedom and emancipation for its inhabitants, in which they can invent their lives, liberated from the conventional constraints of a bourgeois family. If we look at it as an element in the architecture of the city of Utrecht then we can see it as a gesture of attention-seeking, which was welcome here at the edge of town, acting rather like the sort of marker that a city gate-post might once have been. If we look at it as part of the development of modernist architecture, then it is a gesture of great importance, marking one of the crucial moments when the artistry of the building was evident, despite the fact that the form of the building did not derive from earlier buildings, but from more abstract ideas. Which of these is the real meaning? They are all real meanings, and not one of them can be attributed directly to the architect. If we were to want to know about what it meant to him, then we would need to immerse ourselves in the literature of theosophy, and learn about Madame Blavatsky's descriptions of the spirit world. These days not many of us are inclined to do so, but even if we did retrieve Rietveld's original understanding of the building, that would not invalidate the other readings, or make them meaningless.

As society becomes more pluralistic and multicultural, it becomes increasingly difficult to understand in advance what a building will mean to the people who will be using it. If an architect and the building's users are from the same social group, then it is more likely that the gestures will be understood in the way that they were intended. However any public building will be used by people with a multiplicity of different backgrounds, who respond to things in different ways. This is not a problem, so long as the responses fall within a reasonable range, but if for example a modern public official were to erect a house that looked and worked like the Brighton Pavilion, whether the money came from the public purse or whether it was borrowed (as it was when the then Prince of Wales built it) then there would now certainly be a public outcry. It is difficult to know what would be made of the oriental styling in a postcolonial context. It could either be seen as a tribute to an important ethnic minority's culture, or as nostalgia for lost empire, but either way it would have powerful overtones now that were not present when it was built. Then it had some overtones that would be indefensible now, but they were acceptable to the people who came into contact with the building in its day. If it were built today, then there would be riots and resignations. Queen Victoria hated the building and all it represented to her. This was not principally on account of the style, but on account of the life that the building was designed to make possible – a life of extravagance and debauchery, which stood at odds with the image of the monarchy that she was determined to project. It was under Victoria that the Palace of Westminster was rebuilt, as an image of rectitude and piety, suited to the kind of government she would have hoped to see. When the Lord Chancellor's suite there was recently refurbished the price seemed to the popular press to be profligate, but if we make adjustments for changes in the value of money, it would have cost no more than it did originally. From the outset the building's duty was to be magnificent, not cheap. That was what was seen as appropriate to its role.

Now, more than in the past, it is necessary for public buildings to justify themselves to the public at large. We still accept that the meaning and value that is perceived by an educated elite has some value, but as the idea of democracy takes hold ever more firmly, it is seen as necessary for the popular audience to have its say. This was shown with great clarity at the award of the Royal Institute of British Architects' Stirling Prize for 2000 and 2001 (and the practice may well continue) when the prize-winning building was chosen by a panel of experts. The awards were shown on television – a quintessentially populist medium – and the television company organized a poll of its viewers to select their favourite building from those shortlisted. What happened was that the popular verdict was announced, shortly followed by the declaration of the 'real' award, decided by expert opinion (which went to an altogether different building). We do not live in a unified culture, and we do not have a single way of determining what we, society as a whole, think is good. It is unusual to compare the results of two competing methods of

10. Falling Water, Bear Run, Pennsylvania (1936–9); architect: Frank Lloyd Wright (1867–1959). It must have taken a great leap of faith to be persuaded that this house could be viable – hovering with breathtaking audacity over a waterfall in the depths of a forest – but even the wealthy businessman who commissioned it as a holiday retreat baulked at Wright's idea of covering the faces of the overhanging balconies in gold leaf. The living rooms feel close to the natural landscape, partly because the sound of the waterfall is inescapable, and partly because rocky outcrops erupt in the main living room. When approached by way of the front door, the house seems to grow out of the landscape, but it is the view from below that is best known. Wright took the reinforced concrete beyond its limits, and the building has sagged and needed substantial restoration work to keep it looking good. It remains a dazzling exploration of the possibilities of what a house can be.

evaluation in a public forum, as one of them tends to undermine the apparent validity of the other. In matters of taste we are less likely than we were a generation ago to bow to expert opinion, which is certainly a good thing by democratic standards, but it is not necessarily good for the art because it can involve a coarsening of judgement, and can be the means of sanctioning philistinism. I know that I would not want to say that the most popular thing was always the best one, but in our society the popular also has power, because it tends to have market forces on its side, and from time to time the rare and extraordinary does find popular acclaim. Then the object in question, whether it is Van Gogh's *Sunflowers*, or Frank Lloyd Wright's Falling Water (Figure 10) is not only a delight in itself, it also confers status on its owner, and therefore if it comes on to the market, its price is high compared with the cost of making it.

The precise ways in which we respond to buildings are variable according to our prior experiences of buildings. Depending on our acculturation, we might be impressed or dismayed by different things, but cutting across all considerations of style and taste, we respond also to the kind of life that we suppose to be implied in a building – whether it feels wholesome or dispiriting, sordid or dangerous, whether it opens up new possibilities, or reminds us of places where we have been happy in the past. We respond to these aspects of buildings, which are not intrinsic in the buildings themselves, as well as to the abstract set of shapes that we see.

Chapter 2
Growth of the Western tradition

Some places are special

In the ancient Greek world, one of the most sacred places was the sanctuary at Delphi, on the slopes of Mount Parnassus. This was where the god Apollo and the nine Muses who inspired artists were supposed to live. It also had other older associations, and had been used as a place of worship from very ancient times, when snakes were considered to be divine. There was not a city here, but buildings accumulated, many of them gifts from the various city-states that made up the Greek federation. People came here from all over the Greek-speaking world in order to consult the oracle: an arcane procedure that involved a priestess inhaling the intoxicating fumes from burning laurel leaves, and uttering a flow of wailing sounds that would be turned into a neat but cryptic prophecy by the attendant priests. An extraordinary set of things was juxtaposed here. On the outside, set in breathtaking natural scenery, there were artistically accomplished buildings, fine statues, and the recreational buildings that belonged in sanctuaries – a stadium and a theatre. But at the core there was a religious mystery that involved the surrender of rationality to wild hallucination. The site was supposed to be the earth's navel, the point at which its umbilical cord had long ago been attached, and therefore in some sense the centre of the world. An ancient carved stone remains, the *omphalos*, which stands up from the ground, tied off with sets of sculpted bandages, evidently in imitation of an earlier stone which would have had real bandages tied round it in solemn ceremonies. The place was special, and was a place of pilgrimage. This meant that by classical times, when the temple dedicated to Apollo was built, the priests at Delphi were unusually well informed about what was going on across the whole of the Greek-speaking world, and would therefore have been in a good position to give political advice. The superstitious practice of consulting the oracle would have been effective in part because the weird ululations were interpreted by people who were highly knowledgeable about current affairs. The buildings here, which include some very fine ones, had various functions – marking the centre of the Earth, housing the mysterious oracle, keeping secure the offerings brought by the various states (and the buildings themselves were offerings) as well as housing visitors and priests, and entertaining them with athletics and dramas.

The most famous of the Greek sanctuaries now is the Acropolis in Athens – a rocky plateau that rears up from the floor of a broad valley. In very ancient times it was a fortified citadel, but by classical times it had become a religious sanctuary. Again, there were a number of buildings here, the most famous of which is the Parthenon (Figure 7) which is famously a building of the highest artistic accomplishment, built with astonishing precision, out of blocks of solid marble, very finely and accurately shaped. This was the artistic high point of the Acropolis. The most sacred building, though, was the Erechtheion, a rather quirky asymmetrical building, which seems to have been pushed into its final shape because it had to take account of various immovable features on its site. The tomb of an ancient king of Athens was here, and so was a scar in the rock that had been made when the sea-god Poseidon's trident, a thunderbolt, had struck the ground when he was fighting with the goddess Athena. The story goes that the ancient city enjoyed the favours of the sea, and of the olive tree, given by Athena, a warrior virgin. When it came to the point at which a decision had to be made as to whose city this was, the two fought for it, and of course Athena won, which is why the city is called after her. At the Erechtheion there was in a courtyard a descendant of the original olive tree that Athena had brought to the city. Also inside there was a folding stool that had been made by Daedalus – the inventor, who had built the labyrinth on Crete, which housed the Minotaur, half-man, half-bull (whose conception Daedalus had engineered). Daedalus was later imprisoned in the labyrinth with his son Icarus, and they escaped when Daedalus made them wings so they could fly away. The story about how Icarus flew too high and came to grief is surprisingly better known than the story of the successful flight that Daedalus himself made. For us this is all plainly mythological, and we do not think of these events as historical facts, but at the Erechtheion there was an ingenious folding stool that had clearly been made by someone. There were other relics of a similar status – very ancient, with mythical provenances – that made the building a remarkable repository of the city's claims to sacred and cultural authority. The natural features of the place that marked it out as sacred were supplemented with portable relics that enhanced its status, and they were housed in a building of exceptional quality that helped to make the high status of the place even clearer.

When a site is revered in this way, it is often seen as necessary to build something expensive and well designed at the site, as a way of showing how important the place is. The cathedral at Chartres is a good example of the same set of feelings and ways of behaving, but adapted into the culture of a different time and place. It was built in France during the 12th century, over the site of a sacred spring that had apparently been a place of worship from long before Christian times. The cathedral was placed over the spring, but its authority was enhanced by the presence of a portable relic: a length of silk fabric that the Virgin Mary was wearing when she gave birth to Christ. It is still on display in the cathedral today, though it no longer has the cultural importance that it had during the Middle Ages. The building that was put up here was extraordinary. There was an attempt to rebuild the church, but there was a fire before the work was completed, and the authorities concluded that this was because the building was not magnificent enough, so it was reconsidered, and the building was finished in an even more extravagant manner. This was one of the first large-scale buildings in 'Gothic' style, with pointed arches and large areas of stained glass windows. It was here that the spire was invented – a really remarkable leap of the imagination at the time. Here it seemed not only technically possible, but also worth the effort, to make a huge neatly finished tapering pile of stones, and hold it up in the air above the town, visible from the farmland for miles around. The idea spread. The spire served no very clear utilitarian purpose, but was a new way of amazing people. The natural scenery at Chartres is pleasant enough, but unspectacular, and the architecture helped to make up for the lack of natural drama by housing the sacred institution in an arresting way. The interior of the church is also remarkable. It took up the idea that had been worked out in Paris by a team of masons working for the Abbot Suger at Saint-Denis. (The area of Saint-Denis is now best known as the place where the Stade de France is located, the arena at which France won the football World Cup in 1998, and it is easy to reach on the Métro.) It is supposed to have been founded at the spot where Denis, the first bishop of Paris, walked to, carrying his head, after he had been executed for his faith on the hill at Montmartre – a vigorous walk for someone in his condition. Again the church there has an ancient foundation, but it was very richly endowed and had high status because it is the burial place for many of the kings of France. It was here that a way of arranging the stone vaults was devised that allowed large areas of stained glass to predominate, shored up from outside by flying buttresses that arc through the air to lean against the building, helping to shore it up. By using these props, a good deal of masonry could be left out of the walls, without disastrously weakening them. They were taken to an extreme in the cathedral at Bourges (Figure 8) which from some angles looks as if it is nothing but flying buttresses. What happens on the inside here is spectacular, as the whole building is flooded with light coming in through the coloured windows. At Bourges the images in the stained glass are particularly clear, and the familiar stories they tell can be recognized and followed as clearly as if they were a comic book with speech-bubbles. Here too the interior space is vast, as there are two sets of aisles running right round the building, with a row of windows letting light into each of them and then another set directly illuminating the central nave. These large vertical windows, together with the stretches of sloping roof in between, stack up together to make a building that is enormously high. It is so spectacularly convincing that, looking at it, one forgets that it is the natural inclination of stones to make low mounds of rubble. Here the stones have been persuaded to leap into the air, and (even more remarkably) to stay there. The point to be made here is that at Bourges we have a completely unremarkable site, on fairly flat ground, that has been turned into something special mainly by building. And this cathedral stands in a tradition of making light-filled spaces that began two generations earlier at Saint-Denis. The abbey church there is a fine and spectacular building, but it is not large compared with the cathedrals at Paris (Notre Dame), Chartres, and Bourges that were built later, so if we study the buildings carefully, paying attention to the order in which things happened, we can see how the ideas developed and were used with increasing confidence and daring. It would not have been possible for an ancient Greek mason to have decided to build something like Bourges. It would have been, in the first instance, absolutely inconceivable, because the ideas would not have been available to him. It depended on various imaginative leaps, each one of which was in its time as great as that involved in inventing the first spire. And then beyond that, even if he could have had the idea, he would not have been able to imagine how on earth it would be possible to build it. Even if he could have done that, he would not have been able to persuade his contemporaries to believe in him and to finance his efforts, which would most likely have led to huge sums of money just ending up as collapsed rubble. Something like the cathedral at Bourges cannot happen overnight as the whim of an individual, but depends on a cultural and technical background that makes it possible to imagine and realize such things. Another point to notice is that the Gothic style was never adopted with great enthusiasm in the south. There is a fine Gothic cathedral at Milan in the north of Italy, but it is isolated, and the churches with pointed arches and vaults in the south of France and Italy tend not to take on the idea of large windows, but retained the flat walls of the earlier Romanesque style, often using these flat wall surfaces for paintings. One reason for this could be that the spaces enclosed by so much glass would overheat uncomfortably in the summer. Bourges is the most southerly of the really glassy cathedrals.

The pilgrimage chapel, the Wieskirche, in Bavaria is from a later date, from the 18th century (Figure 11). It belongs to a different architectural culture, but a similar religious culture to that which produced Chartres. Here, though, the religious community was not composed of highly educated monks, with a concern to embody arcane numerical symbolism in the fabric of the building, but a much more popular band. The church was founded following a miracle witnessed by a peasant. He joined together various bits and pieces from broken carved statues, using leather to make the flexible joints, so the finished figure of Christ is rather puppet-like. It is not a fine work of art, but was effective as a focus for pious devotions, and it was enshrined above the altar of a spectacular Baroque church. It does many of the same things as the Gothic churches did, but by different means. From the outside the building looks quite plain and simple. It is hardly decorated, except around the entrance, and the windows look like straightforward openings in the walls. It is evident from the outside that it is not quite an ordinary building, because it is the largest building around, set among fields, with little else in sight. One might expect that inside it would be more or less a large well-appointed barn. Certainly nothing would prepare the pilgrim for the drama within, modelled on the lavish architecture of palaces of the day. There is gold and profuse ornament, swirling clouds, and draperies that seem to have been caught up in an upward rush of air. Everything is designed as a piece, and expresses movement and fluidity, whilst remaining quite solid and still in fact. Much of the effect is achieved by the use of paint, which is stippled to make the real columns look as if they are

11. Wieskirche, Steinhausen, Bavaria, Germany (1745–54); architect: Dominikus Zimmerman (1681–1766). This pilgrimage chapel, set in the midst of fields, is quite plain on the outside, but inside it is breathtakingly theatrical and seems at first to be little more than an ornamental froth of plasterwork. This initial impression masks a wealth of technical accomplishment and expressive skill. The building marks the end point of the development of a long tradition of lavish architectural effects, based on an underlying idea of classical ornament, and indeed classical columns and entablatures are to be found in amongst

the riot of ornament. The general effect however is to give the impression of a building that has overcome the force of gravity, and the plasterwork looks as if it has been blown about by a great rush of air, causing turbulence in the detail and drift in the whole. Light comes into the building not only from the obvious windows, but also from unseen sources that should have the effect of spotlighting. The theatre is clearly an influence on the design decisions, from the illusionistic ceilings to the plasterwork and timber painted to look like marble. Impressively, everything that was originally in the church was adapted to the same vision, so the pulpit, the lectern, and all the pews are modelled and carved using the same ornamental style and seem as lively and exuberant as the building. When this church was being built, the Abbé Laugier, who worked at the Royal Chapel at Versailles – a building with many qualities similar to the Wieskirche – published a famous and influential essay on architecture, calling for a return to fundamental simplicity and structural clarity in architecture. One can understand why, but nothing else has matched the intense drama of the best Baroque work, which depended on wealthy patrons – the court and the church – with a need for settings for pageantry and ritual. It enjoyed an afterlife in 19th-century theatres.

made of marble, and painted on flat surfaces to continue the architectural effects into illusionist space, so that the limits of the barn-like space become difficult to define. There are columns piled up on top of one another, draped with impressively solid-looking robed figures, supported by impressively solid-looking clouds. The actual shape of the architectural enclosure was made so as to allow this sort of painting to be done. The edges of the ceiling are curved down to join the walls, so there is no definite break between the two that would make a hard line that the eye could fix upon, and could then accurately find the limit of the room. Instead, we are not quite sure whether we are responding to the real volume or the illusion. Even if we try to see the space without its illusions, it is difficult, and to make the effort is certainly to miss the point. Everything here was conceived for the sake of its theatrical effect, so every detail was considered as part of the whole, and there is no room for standard fixtures and fittings. The pulpit seems to float on air in an agitated way, and even the pews are ornately carved so that they seem to go along with the general exaltation of the spectacle. It is a total all-enveloping work of art – the German word for it is *Gesamtkunstwerk*. There is the same concern for precious things and for dematerialization of the architecture as in the medieval era, but it is pursued here in a different architectural language, with different technical means. Behind and beneath all the ornament there is still an idea of classical order – Roman columns and entablatures are in there somewhere, giving a basic discipline, which then seems to have been stretched, shaken, and draped with festoons. It is a style of architecture that developed at royal courts in the 17th century, and was showy in a way that the lesser nobility could not match because it was so expensive to build. It remained popular among the peasantry, for whom it represented a form of escapist glamour. Again it is worth looking back to the Brighton Pavilion, which once belonged to this tradition of glamorous royal extravagance, and which now reaches a popular audience, that has its breath taken away by the whole thing (Figure 3). The particular style is different, but something about the motivation that produced it is the same, and so are some of the reactions to it.

Life, liberty, and the pursuit of happiness

Thomas Jefferson's house, Monticello, has also become a place of pilgrimage of a rather different kind (Figure 12). Jefferson built the house for himself to live in, and it served him well. However it is visited not principally because it made a good house, but because of the other things that Jefferson did such as writing the Declaration of Independence that announced, in particularly sonorous phrases, that America would no longer be a colony but would be a free land. He had an illustrious political career that made him one of the most important founders of the USA. His house however was not the home of a president but of a plantation-owner. It was from here that he ran his estates, which were vast by European standards, and prosperous. Jefferson travelled in Europe and took a particular interest in architecture, designing not only the central group of buildings at the University of Virginia (around The Lawn) but also

12. Monticello, near Charlottesville, Virginia (1796–1808); architect: Thomas Jefferson (1743–1836). Thomas Jefferson is best known for writing the 1776 Declaration of Independence, stirringly calling for the nation to support 'life, liberty, and the pursuit of happiness'. He went on to be the third president of the United States (1801–9). He built a house at Monticello (1770–9), and then extended and remodelled it (1797–1808), and it has the reputation of being the finest house in America of its age. It has a commanding position, looking out over a great fertile plain. Jefferson's accomplishment was all the more surprising because he had no formal training but picked up his knowledge of building while travelling in America and Europe, and his architectural accomplishment was shaped by his meetings with foreign professional architects, so he was engaged with the thinking of the artistic élite in a way that his contemporaries at home were not.

the Virginia State Capitol – hiring some trained professional help in order to have the work carried out properly. The decisions he took about his house say a great deal about him – what he cared about and what he hoped to be. First, this is not a showy and extravagant dwelling. It is larger than many houses, but not large by the standards of stately homes. Moreover it is clear from the whole approach to the design and furnishing of the house that Jefferson did not aspire to make it a sumptuous palace, but was trying for something more sturdy and austere that nevertheless remained cultivated and comfortable. It deliberated avoided flamboyance, and stylistically we could call it Neoclassical, because it belongs with other post-Baroque attempts to go back to the fundamentals of classical architecture. In doing this he was not alone, but in Jefferson's case the ambition is particularly resonant because it echoes his efforts to think through from first principles what a nation should be, and what rules would govern an ideal society. Jefferson's estate can be seen as a microcosm of the new nation, and the house was the estate's seat of government.

The house has many interesting features, where things were thought out afresh, rather than having everything done in the conventional and established ways. By laying out all the main rooms on a single level, he avoided the need for a space-consuming ceremonial staircase, and the stairs in the house that lead up to the private bedrooms are narrow and cramped, making rather a point of their utilitarian character. Jefferson's own bed was built into an alcove that opened into his bedroom on one side and his library on the other. Culturally speaking, the detailed arrangements of the house are idiosyncratic, but the general impression made by the house is very dignified and familiar. The reason for that is that Jefferson chose to adopt the classical language of architecture for his house, and in doing so participated in a culture that traces its roots back to ancient Greece. Jefferson's house has echoes of other buildings in it, buildings that belong to the Western tradition. His design for the Virginia State Capitol was a copy of the Maison Carrée at Nîmes, the best preserved of all the Roman temples

(Figure 13). The central building on The Lawn at the University of Virginia was adapted from another Roman monument, the Pantheon in Rome (Figure 14). We can analyse the possible sources that are combined in his house, or just enjoy it without being particularly well informed about it. Even without any detailed and particular knowledge, we will understand that this is a building with some authority, that belongs to a tradition of high-status buildings with which we are familiar, and which therefore feels stable and authoritative, rather than being confrontational and challenging. The building asserts its claim on the landscape without anxiety or heightened emotion, but calmly as if it is naturally and appropriately a seat of power. Given that the practical politics of its designer were revolutionary, this sort of expression is not to be taken for granted. By describing the house in this way, I hope I make it clear that there is scope for alternative interpretations. If I do not belong to this 'Western civilization' then I may well see things quite differently, particularly if my ancestors previously made use of this land and lived here without claiming to own it. Instead of it seeming authoritative and familiar, it would then seem alien and arrogant. If I were descended from slaves who worked on the estate, then I might see the architecture as symbolic of oppression.

A traditional education in the arts has often inculcated a familiarity with acknowledged masterpieces. Even though 'educated taste' in these matters can be very different from 'popular taste', this does not mean that it need feel forced and affected. For someone who is immersed in a tradition, the response will be felt as a spontaneous and natural reaction to the building in question, even if it is a tradition that has been learnt from books, rather than picked up unconsidered in the course of daily life. Whether the educated or the popular taste gains the upper hand in a given situation has more to do with cultural politics than it does with right and wrong.

Which earlier buildings of the Western tradition does Jefferson's

13. Maison Carrée, Nîmes, France (AD 1–10); architect: unknown. This is a fairly typical temple in the centre of a provincial Roman city, more finely judged than many similar Roman temples, but in its day it would have had no more than local significance. It is now much more significant than that, because most Roman temples have perished, and this one is the best preserved, so it has been much visited and has been important in forming the architectural taste of – for example – the grand tourists of the 18th century. The arrangement is typical for a Roman temple. The single room of the interior would have housed the cult statue, which would have been able to look (as it were) through the open door to the outdoor altar where sacrifices would be made on feast days, as a public spectacle. This room (the cella) is raised quite high above the surrounding street level – about 4 m (12 feet) – and it is reached by way of a flight of steps at one end of the building. At the top of the flight of steps is a row of fully modelled columns, which support the roof above. They follow the 'Corinthian' pattern, so their capitals have an arrangement of conventionalized acanthus leaves, making a showy decorative top to the column. This was a typical Roman choice for a prestigious building, but the columns are unusual for Roman work in being fluted – most Roman columns were built up from cylindrical sections, which were quicker and easier to carve than those with the vertical striations that followed the admired Greek models. Round most of the building the walls support the roof, and there are decorative half-columns which have no functional significance, but which maintain the visual rhythm of the Greek type of temple. Many Roman temples had plain sides, and the expenditure involved in carving these columns gives an idea of the extravagance and prestige of the project.

Monticello call to mind? It is a classic example of a villa in a landscape setting, the symmetrical pavilion with a central entrance through an arrangement of classical columns. They were built throughout northern Europe in the 18th century, and here is Jefferson building his own version in Virginia. The examples that he would have studied would have been mostly Italian, and in books. Jefferson did not travel widely in his youth, and learnt by reading. He taught himself Italian from books, and he owned a copy of Palladio's *Four Books of Architecture* in an Italian edition, calling it his architectural 'Bible'. He also had other illustrated books about architecture, by English architects. When the Marquis de Chastellux visited Monticello in 1782 he said that the house was unlike any other in America, and that 'Mr. Jefferson is the first American who has consulted the Fine Arts to know how he should shelter himself from the weather'. In other words he was working in a tradition of architecture that Chastellux recognized as his own, that of the European élite.

One point to make here is that Jefferson chose to follow the sense of taste and decorum in Palladio's work, and to consider the building with reference to ideas of proportion and balance, rather than try to pile up an exuberant display of pomp and ornament in the Baroque manner. The house is characterized by its simplicity, and it has an air of repose about it that contrasts with the agitation of some Baroque interiors (such as the Wieskirche, Figure 11, or the Brighton Pavilion, Figure 3, which is not normally classified as Baroque, but since it uses all the same devices – combinations of architecture, sculpture, and illusionistic painting – and has much the same effect, I am inclined to think that it is Baroque in a way, even though the architectural detail is a Western idea of the Chinese). Monticello is not copied from a single Italian or English building, but has absorbed the general idea of Palladio's villas and, working with the underlying principles, Jefferson designed a rather original building suited to his own needs, but clearly belonging to the Palladian tradition. In fact what happened is that Jefferson first designed and built an 'English Palladian' house, and then over many years, and

14. The Pantheon, Rome, Italy (AD 118–25); architect: anonymous, but worked under the direction of the Emperor Hadrian. The Pantheon was not a typical Roman temple, but was unique in its design, though it drew on traditional models. Its entrance front for example is not unusual in its conception, though it is larger and more magnificent than an 'ordinary' temple would have been. Like the Parthenon (Figure 7) it had eight columns across the front instead of the more usual six (octastyle instead of hexastyle). The entrance doorway itself is flanked by two niches that once held statues, and remarkably the ancient bronze doors that close off the interior are still in position. The interior is unexpected and spectacular: a circular domed space, with a great coffered ceiling, illuminated from a circular hole in the roof (the *oculus*) that has no covering. The dome is a triumph of Roman engineering achievement, built in concrete and covering a vast expanse. No dome larger than this would be built for well over a thousand years, when Brunelleschi's dome at the cathedral in Florence was made – begun in 1420. Originally each coffer in the ceiling had a gilded rosette fixed in it, making the dome an image of the heavens. One way in which the building was unusual for a temple was in the elaboration of the interior, which suggests that the rituals that went on here would have made use of the internal space more than was usual. It was this aspect of the building that made it so readily adaptable into a church, which happened at an early date, soon after the official adoption of Christianity in the Roman

Empire, and which accounts for the building's remarkable state of preservation. The gilded bronze tiles that once covered the roof were taken away to Constantinople ('New Rome'), the Christian capital founded in the east by Constantine, where treasures accumulated around the Byzantine court as the role of old Rome waned, and the city became depopulated during the Middle Ages.

after he had travelled (particularly in France) it was adapted with French refinements and elegancies, such as the dome. He had seen this arrangement at a grand house in Paris (the Hôtel de Salm) and adapted it for his own use.

Palladio and his *Four Books*

What is this 'English Palladian' tradition? Well, it was inspired by Andrea Palladio, a 16th-century Italian architect, who not only designed buildings but also wrote about them. In 1570, he published four finely illustrated 'books' on architecture, and included woodcuts of his versions of Roman monuments, which were presented not in their ruined state but conjecturally restored so that they looked how Palladio thought they did when they were new. Along with these ancient buildings he included works that had been inspired by them, executed by modern architects such as Bramante and above all by Palladio himself. In gathering together this work, both archaeological and creative, he presented an authoritative compendium of knowledge about ancient Roman architecture and the principles that informed it, together with designs that showed how those principles and ancient authority could be adapted for use in modern buildings, in churches and impressive villas. The treatise was written towards the end of Palladio's career, and he had a wealth of experience to draw on in saying the things he did. He had been a prolific architect, working particularly around Vicenza and Venice. Venice was prosperous mainly because of its trade with the East, on which it had a firm hold. The Venetian state controlled traffic through the eastern

Mediterranean, and its empire was a string of fortified ports that protected and sustained their commerce so that goods could be brought from Constantinople and beyond without being lost to pirates on the way. The ruling class of Venice owned the palaces that lined the Grand Canal in Venice itself, and also had villas on their estates back on the mainland, that they would visit during the summer. The villas are more or less farmhouses, from which the estates were run, and which include in a single building rooms that served agricultural purposes (barn-like attics) and residential accommodation for farmers, farm and domestic servants, and the nobility, who would have a suite of grand rooms with a ceremonial character. Palladio very skilfully designed buildings that combined all these elements into graceful and dignified arrangements of classical forms, so that the whole unified mass of a substantial building took on a rather stately character.

One of his most celebrated villas departs from this pattern rather. The Villa Capra near Vicenza (Figure 15) is on top of a gentle hill, and was not a self-contained dwelling, as it was designed to be used in conjunction with the owner's principal residence in Vicenza. Its principal purpose was for entertaining, and it was within reach of the town. Uniquely among Palladio's designs, it had four identical façades, each with an entrance through a classical porch – a portico – with steps up to it, and Roman-style columns. There is a dome over the central space, and when the doors are open it is possible to see out into the countryside in all four directions, so it seems as if the villa is an extension and completion of the hill. The slope of the ground is continued in the flights of steps, and from the inside one seems to be on a solid raised platform, sheltered by a painted vault. Monticello is sited in the same way, on top of a hill, with just two entrances, likewise through porticoes with Roman-style columns. The hill in Virginia is rather higher – 'Monticello' means *small mountain* in Italian – but there is a similar attitude to the placing of buildings in the landscape. Frank Lloyd Wright for example would never have positioned a building right at the top of a hill, and even Falling Water, which looks so dramatic when seen

15. Villa Capra, Vicenza, Italy (1569); architect: Andrea Palladio (1508–80). Palladio published an illustrated treatise showing his own designs alongside his restorations of some of the great ruins of antiquity, such as the Pantheon (Figure 14). He worked at Vicenza and in Venice, and designed villas and churches for the Venetian nobility, who had palaces in Venice and farmland on the mainland in the province known as the Veneto, which is where Vicenza is to be found. Most of Palladio's villa designs were for buildings that operated as the base for the running of an estate, which made them more or less farmhouses with a few ceremonious palatial rooms that would be used by the lordly family when they visited during the summer months. The Villa Capra is unusual because it was not used in that way, but was set up as a retreat at a short distance from Vicenza, where it sits on a small hill and looks out across the surrounding countryside with varied views in all directions. It was never a principal residence, but was used for entertaining. A typical Palladio villa would have had a portico with columns at the principal entrance, but this building uniquely among his designs, has four, all identical, looking out into the countryside equally on all four sides. In the centre of the building there is a circular room, from which one can circulate freely out into the porticoes and into the landscape.

from below the waterfall (Figure 10) is tucked away in the forest, and approached from higher ground, so it seems to ingratiate itself into its surroundings, rather than command them. It is only once one is inside, or on the lower ground, that the building's spatial drama unfolds.

Palladio's four books are very practical in their outlook, and very clearly written, intended for architects and their patrons rather than a scholarly audience. In England they were taken up by Inigo Jones in the 17th century. He had travelled to Italy and had been won over to Palladio's ways of thinking, and he put up some remarkable buildings influenced by him, such as the Queen's House in Greenwich and the Banqueting House in Whitehall. What is most remarkable about these buildings is that they were erected at a time when the princes of continental Europe were building increasingly elaborate Baroque palaces, whereas in England the greatest Baroque flourishes were still in the future – St Paul's Cathedral by Sir Christopher Wren, for example was not conceived until towards the end of the 17th century, after the Restoration of the monarchy had brought splendour back on to the agenda, and the Great Fire of London had cleared the ground. Inigo Jones's architecture involved simple massing and a concern for the harmonic proportions favoured by Palladio, who, influenced by the proportions that resonate beautifully in music, liked volumes to have simple ratios in their dimensions, so that a room might happily be as high as it was wide, and be twice as long as the width. This would be a double cube, and these are the proportions of the Whitehall Banqueting House that Jones built for Charles I, and outside which Charles was executed. There are Baroque gestures here, such as the flamboyant painted ceiling by Rubens, but the taste overall is austere when compared with that of the court at Versailles.

The English Palladians

Jones's buildings influenced by Palladio were isolated and untypical of their age. English Palladianism is more firmly associated with the

18th century, when it became the normal modern architecture for the time, ushered in under the patronage of the Earl of Burlington, who built a small but carefully wrought pavilion next to his house at Chiswick in west London (Figure 16). He worshipped Palladio and collected his drawings, and set himself up with his close friend William Kent as arbiters of architectural taste. The artistic salon that operated at Chiswick was presided over by Lady Burlington, who was the only person who actually lived in the villa, and was undoubtedly important in seeing that there was a congenial atmosphere at the place, in which ideas could be freely exchanged. The villa became a focus of artistic creativity, which accounts for a part of the building's great influence. Without this influence it is quite possible that the Baroque in England might have flourished for as long as it did in France and Germany. It is possible that Jefferson, isolated in Virginia and learning from books, might have picked up on Palladio's ideas, but he might have been seen as an eccentric individualist rather than a man of taste by Chastellux when he visited. The current of changing taste cannot be generated entirely by a very small group of people – there must have been receptive audience ready to listen to the Burlington circle's ideas – but nevertheless the villa has a significance in architectural history that is much greater than its small size would suggest. Along with the architectural work and the influence of Lady Burlington's salon, the architect Colen Campbell worked to achieve similar ends with his monumental scholarly undertaking, *Vitruvius Britannicus*, which was a three-volume publication that illustrated architectural works that met with Campbell's approval – all of them in a classical manner, and many of them Campbell's own designs, some of them executed commissions, some of them flights of fancy. Burlington employed James Gibbs, who designed in an Italianate manner that evidently suited Burlington well enough, when he returned from his travels, to remodel his town house, Burlington House in Piccadilly. However, he was replaced by Campbell, who persuaded Burlington that he, Campbell, was the more correctly schooled and authentically Palladian architect. (The building incidentally was on the same site, but is not the same building, as the current

Burlington House on Piccadilly that houses the Royal Academy.) Campbell's publications helped to establish and to spread the idea of simple well-proportioned buildings as a model of excellence, always contrasted with the trashy barbarism of the Baroque, which was portrayed as overladen with ornament that distracted the viewer from its neglect of fundamental principles.

Burlington's villa at Chiswick established an idea of fashionable architecture that dominates our view of 18th-century architecture. What did it mean to Burlington and his contemporaries? It should be noticed in passing that it is only in the wealthiest part of society that there were fashions in architecture. Houses are always expensive to build, and finely wrought carefully considered houses built in dressed and sculpted stone were only ever available to the rich, who had retinues of servants to support their domestic arrangements. Most people were not caught up in any concern to live in a fashionable house, but would be content to have a sound dwelling to live in. Inevitably, in understanding what the building would have meant to its designers, we are involved in seeing the world from a particular point of view, that could be characterized as élitist, because it has always been most readily accessible to the people who did not have to worry about making money for basic necessities. The consequences for the working population of being fired with a passion for the arts gave rise to the Romantic stereotype of the starving artist, who finds a way into an élite culture without having the means to support a reasonable level of comfort. Talented people without private means managed to make their way in 18th-century England by having a patron adopt them, though this was not seen as a suitable arrangement for a man of property to make with a woman, and few women managed to establish themselves as artists, except in acting, which was rarely seen as an altogether respectable profession. William Kent was very respectably adopted by his patron Lord Burlington, and became a closely integrated member of the family. Colen Campbell was not, as he had a healthy income from his flourishing architectural practice and did not need to make himself dependent on the earl. The type of projects in

16. Chiswick Villa, London, England (1725); Lord Burlington (1694–1753). Lord Burlington had a Jacobean mansion to the west of London, and was an enthusiastic amateur architect and devotee of Palladio, whose drawings he collected. The villa shown here was built next to the large house, and was an architectural showpiece that was used for entertaining, most famously for entertaining artists, some of whom Burlington supported with his patronage. The villa therefore had an influence much greater than its size alone would indicate. Lady Burlington had her bedroom here, and was the only person who actually lived in the building, which operated as an adjunct to the house (which is now demolished), and she had an important influence on the interiors, as did William Kent (1685–1748) who lived as part of the household and was responsible for the design of much of the furniture and the gardens. In designing the villa, Burlington took his inspiration mainly from Palladio's Villa Capra (Figure 15) and Rocca Pisani, at Lonigo (1576) a villa by Palladio's pupil Vincenzo Scamozzi (1552–1616), which adapted Palladio's design by reducing the number of porticoes to one, and making the central rotunda an octagonal *salone* (or saloon). Burlington followed him in these modifications.

which the two men could engage were therefore rather different, as Campbell needed to have an eye to the business, whereas Kent could experiment more freely and was not dependent on attracting commissions but only on the goodwill of his patron. The fashionable building, whatever its form, had meaning, as it automatically marked its proprietor as belonging to a social élite. It could be said that this is the most important thing to be said about the building, and it is possible that it could be the main reason for wanting to build it. However, for someone like Lord Burlington who belonged absolutely securely to the highest level of society, with or without a fashionable villa, that was not the point at all. For him it worked the other way round: he conferred social status on architecture by taking an interest in it.

The matter of artistic accomplishment works by altogether different means, and can be reached only by acquiring familiarity with culture and by developing skills. Buildings often acquire meaning by artfully alluding to earlier buildings – admired prototypes – as we have seen before. Here there was the model of the Villa Capra, and also a villa designed by Scamozzi, Palladio's pupil, the Rocca Pisani near Lonigo, the design of which was published in Scamozzi's book, *L'idea della architettura universale*, of 1615. Colen Campbell had already built a version of the Villa Capra as Mereworth Castle (1722–5), and the villa at Chiswick has variation from one façade to another, rather than making them all identical. Nevertheless, all the elements in the building have their precedents in either Palladio or Scamozzi, and the building was therefore authoritatively Italianate. Why was that seen to be a good thing? Because at this time the English gentry all knew that Italy was the cradle of the arts and culture, and therefore travelled there if they could. One of the important educational accomplishments that gave a man social standing and ease in polished company was the Grand Tour, usually a visit to France and Italy, made at an impressionable age by way of education. The grandest of the grand tourists would take a retinue of servants and a tutor with them, but they would also meet artists and scholars who were resident in the places they visited. Indeed

Burlington met Kent when he was travelling in Italy. The tour could take years – the point was to absorb the culture, not to cover a great distance. Young men whose schooling had immersed them in Latin literature therefore learnt to appreciate the ruins of Roman buildings, and the splendours of Italian art and countryside. It was also an important part of growing up, and being away from home left them feeling liberated. There was scope for romantic adventures without fear of having to live with the consequences, and they came back with reports of how free and easy the Italian women's sexual morals were. On their return to England they would be expected to find a profession or a role in the running of the family's estate, and adult responsibilities would come crowding in. The love of Italian architecture therefore was part of an association of pleasurable ideas involving youth, freedom, pleasant climates, and carefree living. There should also have been a steady application to study along the way, and introductions to the high society of the places en route, so when they returned they were socially polished men of the world, who carried with them a nostalgia for Italy and antiquity. This aspect of the architecture touched personal memories and experience, and could not be pinned down and codified, but it was certainly present as a spontaneous emotion. The rules that architects such as James Gibbs and Colen Campbell did try to set down were rules that would have produced architecture that looked appropriately Roman, and would produce sentimental feelings in men of the patron class, even when the architects might not have those feelings themselves.

Reviving Rome

Almost the whole history of high-status Western architecture is the story of attempts to revive and recapture the magnificence of the ancient world, principally the ancient Roman world, which had left behind it some spectacular ruins. One of the most spectacular was the Pantheon (Figure 14), the great domed temple that had been built by the Emperor Hadrian, and then later, in the Christian era after Constantine, turned into a church. Palladio published woodcuts of it in plan and section, and Brunelleschi is supposed to have studied it and other Roman ruins when he was trying to work out how to construct the great dome of the cathedral at Florence of 1420. It is well known that the architects of the Renaissance set themselves the challenge of rivalling the work of the ancients, but there is also a good deal of medieval work that had the same idea, though perhaps with different examples at hand. This is particularly clear in the medieval churches that are called 'Romanesque' precisely because they learnt from Roman examples. For example the Romanesque cathedral of St Lazare at Autun in Burgundy has a row of arches running along its nave, leading into the side-aisles, while up above there is a row of smaller arches that act as windows (a clerestory) and bring light into the space. The same pattern of small arches above large arches is to be found in the town's surviving Roman gateways, which are on a rather smaller scale than the cathedral. The scale seems to have been given by the ruins of an unusual Roman temple – a mass of Roman brick and concrete – that towers over a low-lying field just outside the town. Its surface facing has long since gone, so it is a rather ungainly shape of rubble, but it is impressively large. If we combine the scale of the temple with the finished workmanship of the gates, then we have a pattern that can easily be adapted into the cathedral. The nave there is vaulted, which is an idea that was learnt from Roman buildings such as the Pantheon and from the great bathing complexes built by the later emperors. In the 16th century, Michelangelo would adapt the vaulted space of the Baths of Diocletian in Rome into a church, Santa Maria degli Angeli, and from the 11th century new churches were built with vaults in Burgundy, starting with the church of St. Philibert at Tournus (*c.*950–1120). The Burgundian Romanesque churches looked to the great abbey at Cluny as the seat of their authority, and it made use of pointed arches running along its nave. These pointed arches appear unusually at Autun, both in the nave and in the vault over it – in Burgundy pointed arches do not necessarily indicate that the building is Gothic.

We think of great engineering structures as characteristically

Roman. The engineering works included roads, aqueducts, and military structures such as Hadrian's Wall, that went across the island Britannia, from coast to coast. The scale of operations was stupendous, especially when measured against the available resources – no electronic means of communication, no earth-moving equipment larger than picks and shovels, just large numbers of people involved in highly disciplined working groups. Many of these structures were treated as utilitarian, and were made to work efficiently without being expected to have any artistic merits. For example, the Pont du Gard near Nîmes is a spectacular aqueduct that carried a water supply across a steep-sided river valley (with the River Gard at the bottom of it). The bridge was built from great blocks of stone, which were left 'unfinished'. Temporary timber supports were needed in the making of arches, but once the arches were complete the supports were removed and the arches supported themselves, and much more besides. Some of the stone blocks protruded to make supports for the temporary timbers, and when the bridge was completed these protrusions were just left, and remain to this day. The bridge was in the depths of the countryside – it is visited today for its own sake, and because people like to bathe in the river there, not because it is close to a town centre. When it was new it would certainly have amazed and astounded the few people who went to visit, but would have been visited in the way that a new dam might be visited nowadays, as a spectacle but not as an artistic accomplishment. Had it been in a city centre then it would certainly have been given a more polished treatment. By contrast the imperial baths in Rome and the Pantheon were very finely decorated and finished. The basic engineering structures were covered in marble panels, carved ornament and mosaics. This decorative work, that showed the buildings to be of high status, was derived from the temples that had been developed by the Greeks. This can be seen very clearly in a building such as the Maison Carrée at Nîmes (Figure 13) which immediately looks rather like the Parthenon (Figure 7), but there are also differences, and they belong not just to these individual temples but to the groups of temples of which each of these is a representative. So, for example, the Greek temple has columns all the way round, sitting on a platform that has three steps on all sides (rather large steps, calculated for their visual effect, rather than being convenient to walk up – there is a stone ramp at the end of the building by the way in). By contrast the Roman temple has columns only at the front, and a flight of steps only at the front (and these steps are designed to be walked up). The reason for this is that the Roman temple developed from an earlier type of temple that we call Etruscan, which is what the Roman architect Vitruvius called it in his treatise on architecture (*Ten Books of Architecture*) (Figure 17). The name alludes to the ancient days of Rome, when the settlement was a provincial town in Etruria. The means by which it developed its ambitions are lost, but it grew in importance and came to establish itself as the capital of Etruria, before going on to annex the regions round about – first those close at hand, and then most of the rest of the lands around the Mediterranean, and some way beyond. The Etruscan temple according to Vitruvius was built on a stone platform, and had timber columns making a porch at the front. Its walls were made of sun-dried bricks, which turn soft if they come into contact with water, and can wash away. That is why the stone platform held them up above the level of the ground, and why the roof was made to overhang. The columns were spaced much further apart than in the Greek temple (proportionally further apart, that is) because both they and the beams spanning between them were timber. These temples were quite small in size, and the timber and mud-bricks were perishable, whereas the Greek temples, by the time the Romans came into contact with them, were monumental in scale and built of stone. Not only that, but they had developed a very precisely codified system of sculpting the columns and beams, which developed over a long time and became an exacting set of proportions and adjustments, so that for example the columns were modelled with ridges in them (flutes) that were cut on site so that they would not be damaged in transport, and the columns and flutings tapered so the top of the column was narrower than its base. What is not obvious at first is that the taper does not follow a perfectly straight line, but bulges out very slightly from where that

17. Model of Temple of Juno Sospita, Lanuvium – Etruscan temple, according to Vitruvius (5th century BC). The building shown here is a model made following the description of an Etruscan temple given by Vitruvius in section 7 of the fourth of his *Ten Books of Architecture*. It is therefore a Roman architect's idea of the ancient type of Roman temple, before the days of the empire. The walls of the cella were made of sun-dried mud-brick, which is vulnerable to water. Therefore the building was raised up on a stone base, to keep the walls clear of ground water. The columns were of timber, and the buildings were not large by later standards, and the spacing between the columns is shown as much wider than would become characteristic later on. Then the building would have been in stone, which needs sturdier proportions because although it is very strong when downward pressure is applied, it will crumble easily if it is pushed sideways or bent. The roof was given a wide overhang, again to protect the walls from water – this time from falling rain. There are three rooms in the cella, arranged across the podium. This is the type of temple that the Romans built before they had learnt to emulate the Greeks' masonry and artistry in making monumental buildings.

straight line would have taken it. This bulging (which is called 'entasis') was carefully worked out, and was supposed to make the columns look right when seen by eye – without it there is apparently a tendency for the columns to look as if they grow slightly thinner than they should be in the middle. The Greeks, it can be seen, lavished attention on their temples, or at least on the important ones such as the Parthenon, which was decorated discreetly with fine sculpture. There was not only the cult statue inside the temple, cast in bronze and covered in gold and ivory as was traditional. It was made by Phidias, who was also responsible for the celebrated statue of Zeus at Olympia (which is always listed, along with the Pyramids, as one of 'the wonders' of the ancient world). These statues are now lost, but most of the marble sculptures that decorated the Parthenon survive (many of them in the British Museum, where they are known as the Elgin Marbles). It was a building of enormous prestige, and it impressed the Romans, who adopted the Greek architectural language, simplified it, and applied it to the buildings that they built across the whole of their vast empire, making this classical language the most widely used system of decorating buildings across Europe, North Africa, and the Middle East.

So, going back to the Maison Carrée at Nîmes (Figure 13) which is the best preserved of the typical Roman temples, we can see a cultural memory of the old Etruscan temple, overlaid with the sophisticated architecture of the Greek temple. There is an enclosed room at one end of the platform in which the cult statue would have been, looking out through the doorway to the public altar where sacrifices were made. The outside of the wall of this room (called the 'cella') however is sculpted to remind one of the row of columns that runs right the way round a Greek temple.

Memory

Buildings can carry in them cultural memories of the architecture of the past, and when there has been a need to give a sense of decorum or authority to a building, one of the ways that has been used most frequently in Western culture is to make the building in a way that recalls aspects of the architecture of the past, often the ancient past. Because there has been continuity in this enterprise, it is possible for a building like Monticello, that was built in a remote spot, with knowledge gained from a limited number of books, to resonate with a whole tradition of buildings going back to ancient times. Each time that architecture's classical language has been revived, different aspects of it have come to the fore as being its crucial aspects, and so it has been reinterpreted in a great many different ways and come to mean many different things – some of them completely incompatible with one another. For example, Albert Speer made use of a version of classicism for the Nazis' projects for Berlin, and we see that version of classicism as looking totalitarian and oppressive, but Jefferson's classicism at the University of Virginia looks benign and expressive of freedom and optimism. The classicism of ancient Greece is often presented as emblematic of democracy, as the idea of democracy was invented in Athens; but when it was used by the Roman state it was expressive of a different kind of order, and became something like a multinational company's 'corporate identity' programme. There are sometimes claims that classical architecture has escaped the vagaries of time and culture, and represents a set of forms that has eternal validity. This is a mistake, because although the forms have remained more or less the same their meaning has shifted dramatically over the centuries, so that what it meant to build in a classical manner in the 5th century BC is vastly different from what it meant in the 3rd century AD, and different again in the 16th century. We always see buildings against a background of buildings that we have seen before, and this influences what it is that we feel about the buildings – indeed it means that we notice different aspects of the buildings. The forms of the buildings might remain more or less the same, but we would see them as different architecture from age to age, from culture to culture, and even perhaps from person to person, depending on what our experiences have been, and what it is that we know.

Chapter 3
How buildings become great

Some buildings are special

Some buildings are more important than others. It would be unthinkable for example to write a book about ancient Greek architecture without mentioning the Parthenon (Figure 7), but the Temple of Aphrodite on Kythera could be missed out without the study necessarily seeming incompetent. It was an important temple in its day, but its ruins are not now visible. In fact the remains of genuine ancient Greek temples are rare enough for it to be possible in a book-length study to mention all of them, or at least all of those where excavation has restored the impression of a substantial building on the site. In the ancient world there were far more temples, some of them perhaps in perishable materials that have vanished without trace. The passage of time has reduced the number to something manageable. There are times and places where even less has survived. For example in Anglo-Saxon England (the period between the departure of the Romans and the arrival in 1066 of the Normans) most of the buildings were made of timber, and they have rotted away leaving little for anyone to find. The buildings that do survive were – unusually – built in stone, and they survive in fragments, because they have been extended or rebuilt over the years. Houses on the whole were not built in stone, but churches sometimes were; and where the church was part of a settlement that thrived and grew, the church was remodelled or rebuilt at some point during the thousand years and more that have passed since then. The few Anglo-Saxon buildings that we know are therefore churches from settlements that were at their most important a thousand and more years ago, so civic pride never took over to build a more magnificent Gothic church. In recent decades the knowledge of buildings has been supplemented by information inferred from the remains of timbers that have rotted in the ground. Rotted timbers change the colour and consistency of the earth that has claimed them, and if the site has not been built over in the mean time, or ploughed with a deep modern blade, then it is possible to guess what the buildings might have been like. So, if we are trying to put together a picture of Anglo-Saxon architecture, we find that the positions of discoloured samples of earth are important evidence for us, and we would not dream of ignoring a surviving house, if one were ever to be authenticated. Historically it would be sensationally important, even if it were an unprepossessing little building.

If we are trying to write a history of modern architecture then we have exactly the opposite problem. There is too much of it to be able to mention everything, and almost everything in fact has to be left out. In a large modern city the largest modern buildings are likely to be commercial – office blocks, shopping malls, multi-storey car parks, and so on. These buildings tend to be edited out of the picture presented in an architectural history, because the buildings do not seem to be culturally significant. There are rare exceptions, like the Seagram Building in New York (Figure 18) which has an unusual status, for reasons that will be explained. Even buildings of great prominence and visual interest (like the Philadelphia City Hall) do not have a wide enough cultural significance to justify their inclusion in a traditional overview, whereas a small house like the Schröder House (Figure 9), tucked away inconspicuously out of the centre of Utrecht – itself a much smaller city than Philadephia – is one of the best known buildings of the 20th century. Among architects it is without question the best known 20th-century building in the Netherlands. In fact among architects outside the

18. Seagram Building, Manhattan, New York City (1954–8); architects: Mies van der Rohe (1886–1969) and Philip Johnson (born 1906). Mies van der Rohe was an architect of great seriousness, who was head of the experimental design school, the Bauhaus, in Berlin. He left Germany during the 1930s and moved to Chicago, where he developed his concern for carefully considered steel-frame buildings. His earlier American commissions were in and near Chicago, and included a startlingly transparent steel-frame house for Edith Farnsworth (1945–51) and a pair of apartment buildings overlooking Lake

Michigan, 845–60 Lake Shore Drive, Chicago (1948–51). Here too the outer skin of the building is all glass, subdivided by an absolutely regular steel grid. The Seagram Building was a far more prestigious project, both because of its prominent site and its lavish budget. The glass here is bronze-tinted, and the vertical mullions between the windows are dark bronze. Instead of making the building step back from the pavement line on its upper storeys in order to conform with the building codes, the building makes the extravagant gesture of devoting a good deal of the site to a public open space, and then the building is taken up vertically from the edge of the plaza to the top, without breaking the lines of the mullions. In a city where the price of land was lower, the gesture would have been less sensational and more easily imitated. The building has been seen as authoritative, as showing how to shape a classic steel-framed tall office building, and it has been much imitated, without its mystique being undermined.

Netherlands it is probably the best known building of any age in that country. And this is despite the fact that in central Utrecht, in a prominent position, there is a spectacular post office, dating from about the same time. It is adventurous in its use of materials, making the traditional Netherlands bricks into a series of parabolic arches with glazing between them, so the post office's central hall is flooded with light in a spectacular way. It is a more prominent building, more technically accomplished, and its interior is just as striking, and yet only a specialist would know who designed it, and it is seen to be of only local interest.

Prestige and pleasure

Cultural prestige is at work here. We tend to feel that there is no need to give an account of ordinary things, because their ordinariness means that they are not worth our attention. We can focus on only one thing at a time, and so it makes sense to focus on the special things that stand out from the crowd. Therefore we pay attention to the Parthenon and the Sydney Opera House (Figure 19) but the homes of ordinary Greeks and ordinary Australians do not feature in the architectural history books, even though we would

19. Opera House, Sydney, Australia (1957–73); architect: Jorn Utson (born 1918). The Danish architect, Jorn Utson, won the commission to build Sydney's opera house in an international competition in 1957, on the basis of some vague but graceful sketches. The design changed as it developed with the engineers Ove Arup and Partners, as they worked with the architect to find a way to realize the ideas. The saga of the building's construction is extraordinary, and well before it was fitted out internally it had become the most often used symbol of the Australian nation. The building's lower levels are housed in an almost windowless mass, jutting out into Sydney harbour, looking like a land mass that makes a plinth on which to display to the photogenic tile-covered concrete shells that house the auditoria.

certainly learn a good deal more about how life is lived in these places if we were to study the dwellings. Where ancient Greece is concerned not much remains of the houses, and it is not possible to say with any great certainty how they were used, but there are now attempts to guess, whereas for most of the time that antiquity has been studied, it did not seem to be a question that was worth raising, given that there seemed to be so little evidence to go on. Looking at a home in a modern suburb of Sydney would not give the same aesthetic pleasure as would looking at the Opera House, but it would tell us something about the kind of life that is lived in the culture that produced the Opera House, and would make the fact that it was built seem all the more clearly remarkable – and remarkable it certainly is. There are numerous cultural and practical reasons why it is unlikely that the place would ever have been built. Internationally the Australians are more famous for their love of surfing and barbecues than for their love of opera, and yet a great international competition was held to find a design, and it was won by a Danish architect, Jorn Utson, with some evocative sketches. He did not know how to build the design that he proposed, and the design changed significantly in order to make it possible. It was always an expensive project, but because it was experimental and innovative, the costs escalated unpredictably, and new sources of funds had to be found (a lottery was set up to generate the money). The architect was shot at, and was dismissed, and someone else was brought in to finish the building off and find a way of making the astoundingly expensive volumes work for the staging of operas. Now that it has been built and has settled into the cultural landscape of our times, we treat it as if it were an almost natural wonder of the world, and it is used as a way of symbolizing the whole continent of Australasia in images that circulate around the globe. It is one of the most remarkable of modern buildings, yet it sits rather unconvincingly in histories of modern architecture, because it is difficult to tell a story about a line of development that runs through this project. It seems remarkable and unique, and does not obviously lead on to the next chapter in the story.

By contrast the Seagram Building in New York does exactly that (Figure 18). It was designed by Mies van der Rohe, who had been the last director of the famous radical German design school the Bauhaus. During the 1930s, with the Nazis' rise to power, many people left Germany and went to live in the USA. They had different reasons for doing so. Some knew that their lives were in danger. Mies tried to stay in Germany, but found it impossible to produce the architecture he was intent upon, because Hitler took an interest in design and decided to encourage a more traditional type of architecture, and modernist buildings were suppressed as un-German. With some difficulty therefore, Mies uprooted himself in mid-career, and moved to the USA, settling in Chicago, where he became Professor of Architecture at the Illinois Institute of Technology, whose campus he designed. (Walter Gropius, the first director of the Bauhaus, had made a similar move, and became Professor of Architecture at Yale.) Mies had great personal authority and played on it to the full. His artistic aim was to iron out the role of personal idiosyncrasy and develop building types that expressed their steel-frame construction in a rational manner. The tall buildings in Chicago all had steel frames, but the earlier ones were decorated with historical ornament in order to give them a veneer of cultural respectability. The process is exactly parallel with the way that the Romans covered their daring new vaulted structures with traditional Greek architectural decoration. For example the *Chicago Tribune* Tower, which was designed by Raymond Hood as a conspicuously beautiful building, was covered in stone and had Gothic ornament, so it made a good architectural show and stood comparison with the monumental architecture of the past (Figure 20). Indeed its proprietor invited such comparison by embedding fragments of stone chipped off illustrious buildings around the world. It is to be hoped that they are not all authentic, and that the original monuments were not damaged in order to give up these souvenirs, which are labelled as coming from such places as the Pyramids at Giza, and the Taj Mahal. What these fragments of stone do is to remind us to look at the building in comparison with the great accomplishments of the past. In contrast with the *Tribune* Tower, Mies avoided any forms of historical ornament and tried to make his buildings look as if they were made of little more than the steel frame that did in fact support them. This is more complicated than it sounds, and Mies was famous for designing in an artful way that made the finished appearance look very simple. 'Less is more', he would say; and he inverted the traditional saying 'the devil's in the detail', which means that grand ideas often don't work out because some minor technicality gets in the way. Mies said: 'God is in the details', meaning that what makes a building special is that its minute parts have been well considered and perfectly resolved. Mies established the pattern for the modern tall building first of all in his Lake Shore Drive apartment buildings in Chicago, and then in the Seagram Building in New York, which was much imitated in the following years as a model of no-nonsense corporate glamour. That is why in retrospect it looks rather boring in photographs – because of the influence it had, it just looks like a normal office building. In fact it is a good deal more special than that, not only because it was the first in the line. There is bronze-tinted glass in the windows, and the crisp dark mullions that run right up the building are also bronze, and the whole building looks rather dignified and inscrutable. It was a very expensive building, which has meant that its imitators have tended to produce noticeably inferior versions of the original, but the reason for its historical importance is not so much what it is in itself, but that it had a huge influence and spawned so many imitations. That it why it seems culturally important and why it is always mentioned in architectural histories. By contrast the *Tribune* Tower has probably been admired as much, but it has been imitated very much less, and so it cannot be said to have had so decisive an influence. It was an admirable building, but it did not change the way in which architects saw the office building; therefore it has less historical significance, even though it might (arguably) be a finer work of art. The buildings that we tend to call 'great' are those which change the course of events, so they mark out the next chapter in the story that is being told, and for that reason in retrospect they always look 'ahead of their time'. This is not at all the same thing as supposing that buildings that try to look futuristic are historically important. It is impossible to tell in advance which way things are going to develop, so we cannot always predict which buildings are going to be the historically important ones. It is necessary for them to have some degree of accomplishment, but there are so many buildings around that it would be impossible to tell a story that included even all the reasonably good buildings.

20. *Chicago Tribune* **Tower, Chicago, Illinois (1923–5); architects: John Mead Howells (1868–1959) and Raymond Hood (1881–1934). In 1922 the proprietor of the** *Chicago Tribune* **organized an international competition to find a design that would make the finest office building in the world for his newspaper's headquarters. It attracted entries from prominent architects around the world, and there was a touring exhibition of the entries, so the winning design, by Raymond Hood, was immediately well known and influential. It was on a prominent site in Chicago, a city that is built on absolutely flat ground,**

which makes almost every site seem rather neutral. The tower is on the city's main street, Michigan Avenue, close to the Chicago River, the city's only natural feature, with a plaza between the building and the river. The design put everything into the idea of making the building tower, and made use of Gothic ornamentation, in order to make the whole building look as if it is soaring up to the complex arrangement of masonry that makes the distinctive crown – modelled on the 13th-century Butter Tower at Rouen Cathedral, but very much larger than the original. The building's steel frame made it possible, but it is nowhere visible, because it is covered in limestone. It is therefore a technically advanced building that was stylistically conservative. Looking to historic buildings to give an idea of soaring verticality took Howells and Hood clearly enough to the Gothic cathedrals, where this had been an aim. A less inspired sort of Gothic had also been the style adopted by Cass Gilbert for the Woolworth Building in New York, which was the tallest building in the world at the time of the competition. Howells and Hood had first met while studying at the highly traditional École des Beaux Arts in Paris, and Howells set up practice in New York, establishing a reputation such that he was one of the ten American architects invited to enter the competition. He enlisted Hood's help, and Hood is generally remembered as the building's designer. He was certainly the more flamboyant character, and at the time of the competition was living deeply in debt. When the firm won the competition, Hood's wife Elsie borrowed the cheque, hired a taxi, and took it round New York to show to the various creditors.

Towards a new architecture

In the 19th century there were calls to invent a new architecture for the 19th century, that did not involve dressing buildings up in styles derived from the buildings of earlier centuries. Why couldn't there be an original '19th-century' style? Viollet-le-Duc for example argued that the new architecture would derive from the new ways of constructing buildings. It did not happen convincingly until the 20th century was already under way, and people like Mies and Le Corbusier devised ways of making architecture look as if it had shaken off historical ornament in order to adopt a modern way of doing things, using new materials – the steel frame and the concrete slab. It seemed as if they had managed to fulfil the 19th-century prophecies, which were by then deeply ingrained in the culture of architecture. Their ways of thinking became mainstream among architects during the middle part of the 20th century. The architecture of the generation before them is particularly interesting, because people then were trying to reinvent architecture without it having settled into the path that became orthodox modernism, from which point everyone seemed to reach a consensus about how things should be done. Le Corbusier's masterstroke was to claim that the machine had taken over from the traditional craftsman, and that therefore mass-produced objects were legitimate style-icons. At the Paris Exposition of 1925, he designed a little pavilion, 'le pavillon de *l'Esprit Nouveau*' (the New Spirit) – named after the journal *l'Esprit Nouveau* in which Le Corbusier published his manifesto-like writings. The pavilion was supposed to be a prototype apartment for a vast city composed of many such units, stacked up into towers. He furnished it with mass produced furniture, along with Cubist-influenced paintings that he had painted himself. If it looks rather plain and routine now, then that is a measure of the influence it has had. It stood in marked contrast with the most sustained efforts of the previous generation, such as Victor Horta and Hector Guimard, who developed the Art Nouveau style, based on plant forms. Horta's work in particular involved painstaking craftsmanship – the elaborate swirling shapes sometimes looked as if a building and its furniture had softened and slumped, and sometimes seemed to be sending out tendrils of fresh growth. Timber and stone did not naturally come in the right shapes, which had to be carved, so Horta and the people who worked in his studio made plaster models of the novel forms, and then they were copied by the joiners and masons working on the building. This was an expensive process, so Horta's version of the Art Nouveau was initially only for the super-rich who could afford it – the aristocracy in the then-new Belgian state, who wanted to patronize a new architecture as a Belgian national style. Hector Guimard is best known for the entrances that he designed for the Paris Métro, which have droopily heavy-looking flower heads, with dull red lights that glow mysteriously. They seem to beckon the traveller into a dreamworld, rather than into an efficient transport system, but in their fabrication they were highly rational and depended not on individual craftsmanship but on repeated castings in iron from moulds. The imagery may look soporific, but the means of production was efficient.

This use of mass-production methods in architecture will have helped to prepare the way for Le Corbusier's exhibition of mass-produced furniture, but in the avant-garde circles in which Le Corbusier moved another crucial influence would have been the *provocateur* Marcel Duchamp's practice of exhibiting ready-made objects of mass manufacture in an art-gallery setting. He started doing it in 1914, with a rather striking bottle-drying rack, but the most famous of his 'readymades' was the white ceramic urinal that he exhibited with the title *Fountain* in 1917. Today the most startling thing about the sculpture is the date, 1917, and the tabloid press is still shocked when contemporary artists do rather similar things, now securely within the fold of the art establishment. Duchamp's urinal, or 'fountain', has an architectural counterpart in a prominently placed white ceramic wash-basin, in the hallway of Le Corbusier's Villa Savoye of 1928, where it seems to have some ritual significance, as if it is a holy water stoup. The mass-produced object is in each case used for its sculptural effect, and its unconventional positioning makes it gestural. It is clearly no accident that it has appeared there, but it makes no common sense. One is invited to see it as a gesture belonging to the realm of art and high culture, rather than to the lowly realm of practical utility, in which each object originated. It was part of the point of these objects that they were mass-produced and impersonal, cultivating a machine aesthetic, whereas with Guimard's decorative panels the machine production was not the point, it was just the most effective way to produce the panels at a reasonable cost. Indeed Guimard's panels were not standard-issue productions, but were carefully designed by him, and then produced in limited quantities as necessary for his building designs (but no one else's). Indeed one of the ways in which Guimard's designs for the Métro are interesting is that, despite their striking originality, they are all virtually the same,

21. Métro entrance surrounds, Paris, France (1899–1905); architect: Hector Guimard (1867–1942). The first line of the Paris Métro opened on 19 July 1900, and from the outset was entered by way of the portals that Hector Guimard designed for them as a young man – he was 32 years old when he was given the commission. He had visited Brussels and seen Victor Horta's Hôtel Tassel (1892), which had translated the fashionable Art Nouveau style into architecture. In the Métro stations, Guimard translated the style into prefabricated cast iron, and the portals would appear in their neighbourhoods with great rapidity, so that they seemed to have erupted from under ground overnight. Some of the portals had glass canopies, others did not, but they used standardized parts. There was an outcry in the press when these buildings appeared, and after the vogue for the Art Nouveau had passed, the portals were removed rather than repaired. Between 1927 and 1962 all but two of the original stations were dismantled, the remaining ones being at the Porte Dauphine and Abbesses. Many of them have now been replaced with reproductions.

and clearly the entrances to the underground transport system were imagined as a 'type', rather than as unique individual creations. While Le Corbusier and Mies van der Rohe made it clear that they were interested in developing new types of dwelling, and steel-framed buildings, one associates Guimard's idiosyncratic forms less readily with a rationalist programme of building production. Nevertheless it is plain that these buildings were as efficient and as rational as the transport system they led down to, even though that is not what the building expresses.

The artistic vision seems to be that the Métro is a sensuous dreamworld, and it certainly has an air of being set apart from normal life as we know it above pavement level. A journey on the Métro is framed as a descent to the underworld, from which we return like Orpheus. That does not stop it being a practical transport system, but the practicality is not what the architecture expresses, whereas by contrast Norman Foster's design for the Bilbao subway system makes it as rational as possible, trying to conserve the passengers' sense of direction on approaching the underground platforms, by having very direct links from the pavement, turning few corners on the way. By contrast the Paris Métro has labyrinthine passages that connect its lines, and the traveller is certainly in limbo, which further enhances the associations with the unconscious and perhaps accounts for the fact that it keeps playing a role in Parisian narratives, from *Zazie dans le Métro* by Raymond Queneau (1959), to Jean-Pierre Jeunet's *Le Fabuleux déstin d'Amélie Poulain* (2001).

Back to basics

For the avant-garde architects of Guimard's generation, nature was the usual starting point. In Glasgow Charles Rennie Mackintosh produced intense flower drawings and landscapes, while his architectural work made use of sinuous lines and geometric figures. In Chicago Frank Lloyd Wright developed his 'prairie house' type, with wide overhanging eaves, that was supposed to echo the wide flat horizons of the prairies, though the buildings themselves were in the Chicago suburbs. In Barcelona Antoni Gaudí developed his own highly idiosyncratic way of dealing with buildings, studying bones and beehives along the way. The most ambitious of his buildings was the church of the Sagrada Familia, with its strange stalagmite towers, which he left incomplete at his death (Figure 22). They were all trying to reinvent architecture from first principles, and to find a new way of doing things that responded to new ways of living, and new ways of building. Stylistically they are quite different from one another, and it does not help to understand them by saying that the work should all be called by the same name (Art Nouveau, or whatever) but what they had in common was that they were designing individualistically, and evidently striving for originality. Previous generations of designers had habitually appealed to some idea of 'correctness' to give their work authority. The buildings would look like the admired models from the past, which would be refreshed with individual creative thought, but always working within an established framework of decorum. Even radical change could be authorized by appealing to precedents, if the architect looked to the distant rather than the recent past for the buildings that would be held up as exemplary. In Florence at the beginning of the 15th century, at the start of the Renaissance, the architecture that was all around was medieval in character, and adventurous architects such as Alberti and Brunelleschi brought about change by focusing attention on Roman architecture. In the mid-18th century, when Baroque architecture was at its most sumptuous and exuberant, there was a call for a return to simplicity and the expression of fundamental constructional principles. That appeal was made in the first instance by Marc-Antoine Laugier, a priest attached to the chapel at Versailles, which was more Baroque and excessive in its decoration than anywhere else on Earth. In 1753 he published an essay in which he imagined a primitive hut, made out of trees that were still growing in the ground, as the origin of monumental architecture. As the century progressed, and archaeological excavations produced better knowledge of the monuments of ancient Greece, it became possible to make an

22. Expiatory Church of the Sagrada Familia, Barcelona, Catalonia, Spain (begun 1882); architect: Antoni Gaudí (1852–1926). This is not Barcelona's cathedral, which is a fine medieval building in the heart of the old city, but a project initiated by a Barcelona bookseller, Josep Bocabella, who directed the efforts of the Association of the Followers of St Joseph (founded 1866) which grew to have half a million members, including the Pope and the King of Spain. The project's first architect soon parted from the project, and Gaudí took over from 1883, when work had barely reached ground level. The church is being built slowly, from private subscriptions, and is still incomplete, but work continues, following Gaudí's general intentions. Gaudí's idiosyncratic and striking sense of form was grounded in a profound understanding and rethinking of structural principles, and of practical building techniques.

appeal for the revival of Greek taste in the name of turning towards purity and simple elegance. And then again in the 19th century, when classical architecture was normal, and other styles were used for exotic special occasions, Gothic architecture was revived, especially by Pugin who presented it as a truly Christian architecture, uncontaminated by association with a pagan past (Figure 5). In each of these examples a change in current taste and practice was brought about by making an appeal to the architecture of the distant past, and by making a break with the architecture of the immediate past.

One way in which to make a reputation as an architect is by producing work that is in some sense original, so that it is immediately apparent whose work it is. Gaudí's architecture would be a case a point. No one else has ever put up buildings quite like his. However it is not the case that the more original a building is, the better it is, or the more worthy of attention. The Parthenon is a building of the highest quality, but it looks very like all the other Greek temples of its age and it would not have been a better building if it had departed more radically from that type (Figure 7). Having said that, it is not without originality: the building was not simply a repetition of earlier temples. For a start it is larger than most, and made of better stone, and its decorative sculpture was freshly considered and very well executed. The building is unusual in having eight columns across the façade instead of the usual six, and in being made with optical corrections, the effect of which is perhaps barely noticeable, but the shaping of the stone demanded more care and skill than was usual, and signals a preoccupation with precise refinement of the type. In addition to the decorative frieze running round the building above the columns, which was usual with this type of temple, there was another frieze running round the outside wall of the inner chamber, visible between the columns, and that had never been done before. So there was no doubt that the Parthenon belonged securely within the tradition of Greek temple building, but it was more magnificent and splendid than the temples that had gone before. It is inconceivable that it would have happened, but just suppose that instead of building the Parthenon, Phidias, Ictinus, and Callicrates had collaborated on a work that had turned out like the Sagrada Familia. How would it have looked to the citizens of Athens in the 5th century BC? It would have looked totally bizarre and barbaric. It would not have showed them that its designers knew or cared about their culture. When they looked at it they would not have seen any of the familiar signs that would have prompted in them feelings of recognition and being in familiar territory. Indeed our word 'barbaric' has its origins in the Greeks' word for foreigners, which tells us what they thought of them.

Familiar and exotic cultures

If we are more appreciative of foreigners and their works than were the ancient Greeks, we are also prepared to read and misread signs in buildings that belong to cultures other than our own. A monument such as the Taj Mahal (Figure 23) is as rooted in its own traditions as the Parthenon, and it can be understood with reference to those traditions, as one of a long line of funeral monuments, which surpasses the others by being unusually extravagant and exceptionally beautiful. The image of the Taj Mahal is circulated all over the world, but when that happens, it is rarely read with knowledge of its local culture. In the international culture of global tourism, the Taj Mahal is presented as an alluringly exotic image of the whole subcontinent of India, just as the Sydney Opera House is used to signify Australia. These images become familiar around the world, and are part of the tourist culture. So it happens that when a traveller in a foreign land manages to track down these well-known sights and photographs them, what happens is not so much a confrontation with something original and unaccountable, as a recognition of something familiar. The classic tourist photograph ('Here I am, standing in front of the Eiffel Tower') is not a way of learning about world architecture – there are clearer photographs with better explanations in the guidebooks – but of having evidence that one belongs to the privileged élite that travels

23. Mausoleum of the Taj Mahal, Agra, India (1630–53); architect: Ustad 'Isa (dates unknown). The famously beautiful mausoleum of the Taj Mahal was built as a memorial to Mumtaz I-Mahal, by her husband the Shah Jehan, Emperor of Mughal India. The architect's name was forgotten, but rediscovered from documentary evidence found in the 1930s. He was brought from Persia, and the design is the refined product of centuries of Islamic tradition. It is the centrepiece of a monumental complex that includes a red sandstone mosque and gardens with plants and reflecting pools. The mausoleum is entirely covered in white marble that gives the building an ethereal quality, whether it is reflecting intense sunlight into its shadows, picking up the subdued light of the moon, or the colour of the setting sun. The sight of the building moves all commentators to hyperbole, and it accumulates unsubstantiated romantic myths.

the world. More people than ever before can travel to the far side of the world, and do so without great difficulty and without needing any very compelling reason for doing so. News and ideas are transmitted round the world with even greater facility and speed, as certain aspects of our culture become globalized. If we want to know more about the Taj Mahal and its significance, then we need to study the architecture of Islamic northern India, and Persia, from where the architect came. If we want to know more about the meaning and significance of the forms of the Sydney Opera House building then we do not find them in the Australian outback, but in Denmark, and perhaps the Mediterranean, where the architect had built himself a house. The cultural influences are not tied to the place in the same way.

The reasons for choosing Le Corbusier as the architect for Chandigarh (Figure 6) are similarly complex. He was not a local architect, but had established himself as a significant figure in Western architectural culture. His culture was in many respects the culture of the departing colonial powers, from which the new state wanted to distinguish itself. By showing that high-status modern buildings could be produced by local workforces, the state showed its aspiration to belong internationally in the modern world. A neoclassical building that looked like the imperial buildings of New Delhi would have been inappropriate, given the state's aspirations. The designs, by being authoritatively modernist, suggest that the state was making a fresh start, but it is an irony that Le Corbusier would not have been commissioned had it not been for the sustained efforts of representatives of the former colonial power (Maxwell Fry and Jane Drew) to persuade both the authorities and Le Corbusier himself that he was the right person for the job. It is very much a postcolonial design, which can command the respect of the former colonials, while presumably satisfying the needs of the local community. In many respects it exactly reverses the attitudes to Indian culture on display at the Brighton Pavilion (Figure 3) where the idea of India is conjured up as an exotic fairyland. At Chandigarh we have an image of India, or more specifically the Punjab, as a modern working state that has a serious role to play.

The Guggenheim Museum in Bilbao belongs very securely in the realm of global tourist culture (Figure 24). It is a building that has had importance in reviving the fortunes of a small city, by making it a place that people from all over the world want to visit. The benefits to the city are much greater than the cost of the building, extravagant though that might seem. The collection of art works that it houses could have been seen just as clearly in a modest and inconspicuous building that excited no one. The cultural tradition to which the building belongs owes little to northern Spain, where it is located, and rather more to Los Angeles, where it was designed. Its form is part of a family of shapes for buildings developed in the remarkable and idiosyncratic studio of Frank Gehry, and it recognizably belongs to his own personal tradition, which has been developing for decades. More broadly, it makes sense in the tradition of the avant-garde, that was developed in the art world, and which makes the building highly appropriate for the housing of works of avant-garde art, which again are the works not of local artists but of internationally recognized stars of the art world. So the museum's collection has more in common with the collections of contemporary art to be found in the great American cities than it does with collections of contemporary art in nearby provincial towns. By participating in the global culture of the international art world, the city is able to cut a dash on the international scene and attract visitors and investment, and the building is successfully assimilated in two cultures (of the artistic avant-garde and of tourism) which in this case work together to bring about that success.

The architect's own culture is something else again. Gehry's compositional sense might have developed by crumpling cardboard and arranging it loosely on a site plan, but there is a huge difference between having some crumpled card glued to a board and having a working art gallery built on a site in Spain. A host of technical

24. Guggenheim Museum, Bilbao, Spain (1997); architect: Frank Gehry (born 1929). Frank Gehry was born in Canada, first moved to California as a student, and then settled and started an architectural practice there, initially making fairly conventional designs. His experimental work, starting with his own house in Santa Monica, has taken him in the direction of designing buildings that have more in common with the traditions of sculptural form than with architecture. The design for the Guggenheim Museum in Bilbao is spectacular and eye-catching, and has helped to draw international attention to a provincial Spanish city, establishing it on the cultural map of the world. The building is constructed with a steel skeleton, clad in titanium tiles, and it seems almost beside the point that it contains gallery spaces for the exhibition of art works. It is the architectural equivalent of a firework.

questions arise, and they must be addressed with sensitivity and skill if the idea is not to be spoiled in the execution. If for example the shapes could not be built, then they would have to be changed, so a way of building them has to be found, which in this case involved making use of a steel frame to form the basic shapes, and then covering it with titanium-coated tiles that could adapt to the curving geometries. It would have been impossible before computers became a routine part of an engineer's equipment for such a form of building to be seriously considered, because the mathematics involved are so complex. The steel and titanium pieces were cut into shape away from the site, in factory conditions, where the work can be done with much greater precision. That they could be brought on to the site and assembled is little short of miraculous. It is a world away from the studio conditions in which Gehry invents the building form. He once made an armchair by gluing corrugated cardboard into a large block, and then modelling it with a chainsaw.

Frames and blocks

Architects who see their building through to construction must take an interest in the processes of building, and often it is that process of building that finds expression in the finished work. There would be an attempt for example to make bricks do the things that are particularly characteristic of brick, by making walls and arches, while steel would be asked to do the things that are particularly characteristic of steel, such as making grid-like frames. A building with a steel frame will usually need walls and windows in order to make it useful, and it is possible to make the walls cover the steel frame and hide it from view, which can make the building look solid. However an architect can make it a point of principle, as Mies did, to arrange the solid parts of the wall in such a way as to make it apparent that the steel frame is holding the building up, while the walls are just acting as non-structural screens. In becoming absorbed in the expression of such niceties of construction, it is possible to design fine buildings that are admired by other architects, but which look to the uninitiated very much like unexceptional industrial work. Even the Seagram Building, with its commanding reputation and its understated monumentality, has never been promoted as a tourist sight, except among architects. In fact the idea of 'expression' here is less straightforward than at first it seems, because the grid of evenly placed verticals and horizontals is not the whole story of the construction. A building also needs cross-bracing in it, to stop the whole structure collapsing sideways in strong winds (and winds are much stronger on the twentieth floor than they are at ground level). Mies did not let these diagonal bracings show, but others have done (for example, Skidmore Owings and Merrill at the John Hancock Tower in Chicago). Also it is problematic to expose steel columns in a tall building, because the structure needs to withstand fire better than steel does by itself. Therefore the steel columns in Mies's buildings sometimes had to be cased in protective material, like concrete. In order to express the structure, he then cased the column in steel, making it look as if the building were held up by larger steel columns. The point to be made here is this: even when an architect decides that a building will express its own construction that does not mean that the process of design takes care of itself. There are many decisions to be made, which are often matters of judgement that could change the building's appearance. Why, for example, does one express the fact that the structure needed to resist gravity, but not that it needed to resist wind? Why not express the fact that columns are protected to make the building safe in case of fire? The occupants of the building might find that very reassuring. The answer surely is deeply traditional. The Western tradition has for over two and a half thousand years found particular value in buildings with columns, and they have been seen as the basis of a building's aesthetic effects. Monumental buildings had large columns. High-status buildings had finely wrought columns, made of good materials. The Greek word for column is *stylos*, which is the root of the English word 'style'. The row of columns around a Greek temple is called the peristyle. A building without columns is called 'astylar', without style.

Tradition and novelty

This tradition has been challenged as attempts have been made to express other important aspects of the building, such as the heating and ventilating equipment, which can amount to a large part of the cost, and be difficult to hide away. At the Centre Georges Pompidou in Paris, for example, the various service ducts and circulation systems – stairways, escalators, and lifts – are made highly visible, threading their way through the structure of the building to give it its particular character (Figure 25). The structure here is handled ingeniously, so that the large columns are mostly hidden within the building, and the structure that is visible in the main façade is hardly more than a network of fine steel, which has the appearance of scaffolding. The building, when it is swarming with people, seems to be little more than a support for the activities in and around it, which is its point. This is architecture conceived as a 'facility' rather than a monument. It is a place where events are made to happen, rather than a determinedly beautiful self-sufficient form. People who look at it in photographs see it as an assembly of girders, reminiscent of an oil refinery, but people who have visited it remember more clearly the journey up the escalator, the views from the top, which are extensive, and the rooftop café, the exhibitions, or the street performers. For such a large and colourful building, it is surprisingly reticent, but it works by such different means than does, say, the Parthenon, that we might wonder whether the same category, 'architecture', can be the right category for both of them.

In fact, though, both buildings belong to the same tradition and have some points in common. Of course there are differences, of attitude and atmosphere, which are so obvious that they hardly need to be pointed out. However each building is an artistic showpiece, that houses art treasures. In the case of the Parthenon, the much-admired statue of Athena dominated the interior space, but the holier relics were housed a short distance away in the Erechtheion. The Centre Pompidou exhibits major art works in changing exhibitions, but the art works to which the most serious

25. Centre Georges Pompidou, Paris, France (1977); architects: Renzo Piano (born 1937) and Richard Rogers (born 1933). The Centre Pompidou is a cultural complex housing libraries, galleries, and related facilities. It was introduced into a run-down area of central Paris (Beaubourg) and had the effect of reviving the area's fortunes as it became a fashionable place to visit. It defies the tendency of this type of building to become monumental, by seeming to be no more than a scaffolding to hold the various lively activities in place. In the early stages of the design, almost everything about it was moveable – even the floors – but in the event that proved to be too expensive an idea to realize. In summer there are usually crowds outside, watching street entertainers in the plaza in front of the building, and a constant stream of visitors going up the escalators, prominent on the main façade, that bring expansive views across Paris into sight as one ascends.

reverence is due are housed a short distance away at the Louvre. Each building presides over an external space, which in the case of the Parthenon was more formally designated a sanctuary, but which in the case of the Centre Pompidou is a well-defined public square. The innermost part of each building is restricted and reserved for quiet contemplation, whether of the statue that embodied a god, or the works of art with their ineffable value. The area outside each building is equally festive. On days of sacrifice, the gods being immaterial beings were well satisfied with the aroma of the slaughtered oxen, and the citizens of Athens would feast on the flesh – a feature of Greek sanctuaries used to be the suites of dining rooms, arranged in stoas. In the Place Georges Pompidou there is street entertainment, and there are cafés. The Parthenon's sculpted frieze depicts a procession, while the Centre Pompidou avoids sculptural decoration, but the visitors enact a procession as they queue and then ascend by the escalators that run across the front of the building. Moreover this procession is in more or less the same place in each building, somewhere between the outside and the inside, in the peristyle of the Parthenon, visible between the columns, and in Paris in a glazed tube visible from the square. It is possible that both buildings look the way they do because of concerns to express the building's construction. There is a tradition (which is questionable) that the Doric frieze on temples such as the Parthenon is a memory of the time when these buildings were constructed in timber, and the geometric triglyph panels represent the ends of timber beams. In the Centre Pompidou the parts of the building are joined together in highly visible ways, so that the assembly of the elements itself becomes decorative. Also it is not incidental that both buildings seem to have well-defined rectangular footprints on the ground: an impression that is less than straightforward in the case of the Centre Pompidou, where parts of the building extend underground beneath the sloping square. It may seem that these points of comparison are trivial, and are less significant than the differences between the buildings, but the point to be made is that there is no doubt at all that we look at the Centre Pompidou with reference to other buildings, whether they be great cultural monuments or oil refineries. The same cannot be said of the Guggenheim Museum in Bilbao, which is to an astonishing degree unlike most other buildings we have encountered in images. It does not look like an authoritarian monument. It does not look like an oil refinery. It does not look like any other art gallery, but as its image becomes more familiar, we learn to recognize it as one. What, then, are we to make of it? Far from being the be-all and end-all of architecture, originality is a mixed blessing, because to be totally original is to be totally meaningless. In fact the building is not meaningless, because it connects strongly with another tradition that is entirely appropriate given the building's function: it looks like a sculpture. We tend to look at it by the standards of sculpture, and are willing to enjoy its shapes for their own sake, regardless of the fact that they do not reflect the way the building is used internally, or articulate the means of contruction. The steel frame is entirely covered, so one need not notice that it is there. The interior spaces are as different from the external envelope as the Chinese interior of the Brighton Pavilion is different from its Indian exterior. Unlike most sculpture, the museum has an interior, but when seen from the outside it has more of the character of a useful habitable sculpture than it has the character of a building. This impression needs to be corrected if one is familiar with Gehry's other buildings, which show a steady line of development that constitutes a personal tradition, in which each new building makes sense as a further step, which it would have been impossible to predict but which in retrospect seems to make sense.

What we experience when we encounter buildings is felt spontaneously, but it is filtered through the culture that we have acquired on our journey to that encounter, and we will have acquired some of that culture deliberately, some of it by chance. The parts that we acquire by chance will be the things that we pick up from the culture that surrounds us, and so will be the result of accidents of birth, and the circles in which we move. This is the culture in which most of us feel most at home most of the time, and in which we live our everyday lives. The most important aspect of the things we encounter in this way is their familiarity. There is room for a little novelty now and again, so that we are not faced with unrelieved tedium, but the familiarity of our surroundings is as reassuring as the predictable attitudes of our friends. We start to worry if someone we think we know well starts to behave in unexpected ways.

Educated tastes

Another part of our culture is that which we have deliberately set out to acquire, in one way or another. It is clear that we can deliberately educate our tastes. It is less clear why we would choose to do so, as at the outset the effort outweighs the immediate pleasures. We must have a conviction that something good will come of the effort that we put into these things. With music for example it is rare to find a piece that sounds best at its first hearing, and if it sounds worse as we get to know it then we are bound to think that it is bad music. We need to familiarize ourselves with the music's sound-world, so that we have a sense of what sound sequences are possible, and then we can listen in a way where we can be happy with our immediate responses, so that one can be prepared for listening to a piece by Mozart by knowing other compositions by him; but familiarity with Mozart's polished elegance would not be enough preparation to be able to enjoy one's first hearing of a piece by Bartok, with complex astringent harmonies and the lively irregular rhythms of Hungarian folk dances. It is only when one is more familiar with his sound-world that the music comes to have the power to move. Similarly with architecture there are buildings that follow recognizable patterns – the most pervasive across the development of Western civilization being the varieties of classicism. There are also regional traditions, and the recent international tradition of modernism and its variants which can turn into individual personal traditions, as in the case of Frank Gehry and other architects who design 'signature' buildings around the world, where part of a building's prestige comes from the fact that it is the work of an identifiable designer, and can be recognized by people who take an interest in contemporary architecture. A city's prestige can grow by collecting such buildings, which show that it has a place in the cosmopolitan world. We can get to know our local buildings by chance, and especially if we use them regularly we can form strong views about them, responding to whether they help us or frustrate us as we try to go about our lives. Without particularly thinking about it, we are probably quietly pleased that these buildings continue to be there, acting as reference points against which to plot our progress through a familiar city. It would be possible for the buildings in question to be quite ordinary, or if my journey to work were to take me through Westminster, then I might find that I was treating national monuments such as the Palace of Westminster in just this way, as local landmarks. Our reactions to the buildings depend as much on our ways of thinking about them as they do on the buildings themselves, providing that the buildings remain reliably in place. But this way of thinking about buildings has only local significance, and would not prompt anyone to make a journey to see the buildings in question. For that we need to be convinced that the building in question is very special indeed for one reason or another. In some cases the building might be extravagantly eye-catching and unlike anything else that we have seen, or – as is the case with the Seagram Building and the Parthenon – be the highly accomplished 'original' example of a widely used building type, which makes it in some way authoritative. They have significance not only because they are fine buildings, but also because they are part of a story that is told about the development of architecture through the ages. The key buildings in that story form a 'canon' – a set of buildings that everyone with a certain level of polite culture might be expected to know. The German word for this level of culture is *Bildung*, for which there is no precise English equivalent, but there is nevertheless still a feeling that one *ought* to know about certain buildings. If I realized in the course of conversation that an architectural historian of towering reputation had not heard of the Parthenon, then I for one would feel inclined to think that there was something fraudulent about the reputation. Some buildings are so regularly used as reference points in our culture that not to know them is to show that one does not participate in the culture. And the culture in question here is not local but international – which is not to say that it is uniform everywhere. If I look back at the list of illustrations selected for this book, it is plain enough that I am writing from within a Western tradition. The cottage that is shown in Figure 2 was chosen as a fairly typical example of a low status traditional building, and no one would expect an architectural historian to recognize it with any precision. It is not famous. All the rest of the buildings are well known, with the exception of the Etruscan temple, which is more specialized but necessary for the story that I was trying to tell at that point. Most of the buildings have stood the test of time and have already shown themselves to be useful reference points in the discussion and analysis of architecture. Some personal favourites such as Hagia Sophia in Istanbul and the Kimbell Museum by Louis Kahn have not found their way into the discussion, which surprises me. Had I been from a different part of the world, then my attempt to give an impression of architecture would have included some different examples. I would have had fewer buildings from Western Europe, and my sense of what is central and what peripheral would certainly be different if I were rooted in a different tradition. However, many of the same buildings would certainly have been included in other people's selections: the idea is to give an introduction to a range of buildings with wide significance, and most of them will be familiar to anyone who has taken an interest in the subject. It is possible to imagine alternative canons, based around the telling of different stories about architecture, that would generate a different choice of buildings. That would amount to a radical departure, whereas the aim of this book is to introduce a selection of buildings of acknowledged merit. Once a building has an established place in the canon then it does one no good as a novice to challenge its place there. There is no doubting the merit of the Parthenon or Bourges Cathedral, and if we go round telling people that we're not impressed with them then that stands as a judgement on our understanding, which can be discounted, not on the buildings, which continue to be seen as outstandingly good. This is the means by which fine buildings become great buildings. They cross a threshold and become unassailable, as any attempt to denigrate them simply undermines the credibility of the critic. If one is not impressed with the pyramids, then one had better learn to be impressed by them. Naïve wonder still has a place in our experience, and buildings that make us feel it are certainly to be valued. Gehry's building at Bilbao might do that. The building is striking and fascinating, and does not initially prompt a feeling of recognition, but of incomprehension, which is the root of wonder and exploration. It is however an emotion that we must experience in small doses in our everyday lives, partly because even the strangest buildings rapidly become familiar if they are part of the daily round, and partly because if we wondered too much then we would never get anything done.

Buildings and culture produce architecture

We like to think that the canonic buildings have timeless value, that sails serenely across the vagaries of human histories, but on closer examination this view cannot be sustained. There is no doubt that some buildings have always been valued, but they are valued in different ways at different times. It would be idiotic to argue that the Parthenon, for example, had no great value, but it has been valued at different times because it seemed to express different things, such as the triumph of Athens over her adversaries, or as a symbol of the roots of democracy. The value remains high, but it is volatile. Buildings are solid things, and the properties that they have are inherent in them. Architecture is produced when a building and a culture come into contact, and connect in such a way that something valuable happens. We might be thrilled by it, or calmed, feel challenged or charmed, but if we do not pay attention to those responses and cultivate them, then architecture dies in us, and the built world is an arid place. But once one knows something about architecture then buildings come alive, and it is possible to see unconscious expressions of skill and intelligence at work wherever one goes, possibly set alongside expressions of vanity, greed, and incompetence. We like to see the great buildings around the world as the clearest expressions of one lofty ideal or another. We see them as something imperishable that embodies a fleeting glimpse of eternity, and we will travel across the world to encounter them. But there are also pleasures closer to home, which may be no less intense, involving a feeling of rapport with a place, which may involve a surprising range of the contradictory emotions involved in any long-term relationship.

Timeline

First pyramid: the Step Pyramid of Zoser at Saqqara, Egypt (2773 BC); architect: Imhotep

Great Pyramid of Khufu, Giza, near Cairo, Egypt (2723–2563 BC); architect: unknown (Figure 4)

First wheels with spokes (*c.*2000 BC)

First use of iron around the Mediterranean (*c.*1500 BC).

The Parthenon, Athens, Greece (447–436 BC); architects: Ictinus and Callicrates working with the sculptor Phidias (Figure 7)

Temple of Juno Sospita, Lanuvium, Etruscan temple (5th century BC) (Figure 17)

Invention of the compound pulley, attributed to Archimedes (born *c.*287 BC)

First wheeled vehicles steered by turning front axle (*c.*50 BC)

Maison Carrée, Nîmes, France (AD 1–10); architect: unknown (Figure 13)

The Pantheon, Rome, Italy (AD 118–25); architect: anonymous, but worked under the direction of the Emperor Hadrian (Figure 14)

Romanesque: first post-Roman stone-vaulted church, Tournus, Burgundy, France (*c.*950–1120); architect: unknown

First Gothic: rebuilding of the abbey church of Saint-Denis, Paris (begun 1137); under the direction of the Abbot Suger (1081–1151)

High Gothic: cathedral of St Etienne, Bourges, France (begun 1190) (Figure 8)

First production of crown glass in Rouen (1330)

Renaissance: dome of the cathedral at Florence, Italy (1420–34); architect: Filippo Brunelleschi (1377–1446)

First post-Roman façade using superimposed classical orders: Palazzo Rucella, Florence, Italy (*c.*1455); architect: Leon Battista Alberti (1404–72)

Villa Capra, Vicenza, Italy (1569); architect: Andrea Palladio (1508–80) (Figure 15)

Whitehall Banqueting House (1619–22); architect: Inigo Jones (1573–1652)

Mausoleum of the Taj Mahal, Agra, India (1630–53); architect: Ustad 'Isa (dates unknown) (Figure 23)

St Paul's Cathedral, London, England (1675–1710); architect: Sir Christopher Wren (1632–1723)

Plate glass first produced in France (1688)

Chiswick Villa, London, England (1725); Lord Burlington (1694–1753) (Figure 16)

Wieskirche, Steinhausen, Bavaria, Germany (1745–54); architect: Dominikus Zimmerman (1681–1766) (Figure 11)

Monticello, near Charlottesville, Virginia (1796–1808); architect: Thomas Jefferson (1743–1836) (Figure 12)

Royal Pavilion, Brighton, England (1815–21); architect: John Nash (1752–1835) (Figure 3)

Gothic Revival: Palace of Westminster, London, England (1836–68); architect: Sir Charles Barry (1795–1860) with A. W. N. Pugin (1812–52) (Figure 5)

Early use of cast iron: Crystal Palace, Hyde Park, London (1851); architect: Joseph Paxton (1803–65); designed as a temporary exhibition building

Steam-powered elevator patented by Elisha G. Otis (1861)

First electric elevator built by Werner von Siemens (1880)

Expiatory Church of the Sagrada Familia, Barcelona, Catalonia, Spain (begun 1882); architect: Antoni Gaudí (1852–1926) (Figure 22)

Early use of a cast-iron structural frame: Home Insurance Co. Office Building, Chicago, Illinois (1883–5); architects: William Le Baron Jenney (1832–1907) and William B. Mundie (1893–1939). This is a prominent ten-storey office building.

Eiffel Tower, Paris, France (1889); architect: Gustave Eiffel (1832–1923)
Steel-reinforced concrete devised in 1892 by the Belgian engineer François Hennebique (1842–1921)
Art Nouveau: Métro entrance surrounds, Paris, France (1899–1905), using prefabricated cast-iron panels; architect: Hector Guimard (1867–1942) (Figure 21)
Machine-drawn cylinder glass first produced in USA (1903)
First real skyscraper: Woolworth Building, New York (1910–13); architect: Cass Gilbert (1850–1934). This was the tallest building in the world until 1930.
Chicago Tribune Tower, Chicago, Illinois (1923–5); architects: John Mead Howells (1868–1959) and Raymond Hood (1881–1934) (Figure 20)
Schröder house, Utrecht, Netherlands (1924); architect: Gerrit Rietveld (1888–1964) (Figure 9)
Pavillon de *l'Esprit Nouveau*, Paris, France (1925); architect: Le Corbusier (Charles-Edouard Jeanneret, 1887–1965)
Villa Savoye, Poissy, France (1928–30); architect: Le Corbusier (1887–1965)
Empire State Building, New York (1929–31); architect: Shreve, Lamb and Harmon
Falling Water, Bear Run, Pennsylvania (1936–9); architect: Frank Lloyd Wright (1867–1959) (Figure 10)
Seagram Building, Manhattan, New York City (1954–8); architect: Mies van der Rohe (1886–1969) and Philip Johnson (born 1906) (Figure 18)
Chandigarh, Punjab, India (1950–65); architect: Le Corbusier (1887–1965) (Figure 6)
Opera House, Sydney, Australia (1957–73); architect: Jorn Utson (born 1918) (Figure 19)
Centre Georges Pompidou, Paris, France (1977); architects: Renzo Piano (born 1937) and Richard Rogers (born 1933) (Figure 25)
Guggenheim Museum, Bilbao, Spain (1997); architect: Frank Gehry (born 1929) (Figure 24)

Glossary

Baroque: This is a stylistic development of classical architecture, where the building is overlaid with ornamental work, often including statuary and illusionistic painted murals and ceilings. It developed in 16th-century Italy, and was widespread throughout Europe in the 17th. The most floridly grand style of architecture. See *Rococo*.

broken pediment: a *pediment* with a gap in the middle.

cella: the enclosed room in a classical temple.

CIAM: *Congrès internationaux d'architecture moderne* (international congresses of modern architecture), a series of meetings held between 1928 and 1956, dominated by Le Corbusier, at which resounding declarations were made in an attempt to determine what the agenda for modern architecture should be.

classical: 1. pertaining to ancient Greece and Rome: classical architecture is in a style derived (ultimately) from the architecture of ancient Greece and Rome; 2. specifically of Greek architecture: pertaining to the 5th century BC.

clerestory: A clerestory (pronounced 'clear-story') window is a high-level window, especially in a church.

Constructivism: a revolutionary movement in Russian art and architecture in which abstract geometric shapes predominated, as did the colours black, white and red.

Deconstructivism: This was a term fashionably applied to architecture in the 1990s, deriving from Constructivism on one hand, and Deconstructionist philosophy on the other. It was the name for the style of philosophy was coined by Jacques Derrida, who was little understood. There were two ways to pass as a Deconstructivist; either by designing buildings that looked as if they might be falling apart, or by designing buildings that were accompanied by texts that sounded like high-powered philosophy. In popular usage now 'to deconstruct' means 'to analyse'.

Doric: This was the most severe of the Greek orders, and the first to develop. The other 'canonic' orders were to be called Ionic and Corinthian, but in addition there were idiosyncratic local variants. The Romans extended the range, and they were codified by Vitruvius and then in *pattern books* from the Renaissance.

eclectic: in more than one style; from the Latin word for 'to select', suggesting a range of interchangeable stylistic choices.

entablature: the beam-like part of a classical temple that runs horizontally across above the columns.

frieze: This is part of the *entablature*. In more ornamented buildings it is distinguished by having sculpted panels (in a *Doric* frieze) or a run of continuous sculpted decoration. It is also a horizontal run of decoration applied to a wall.

Gothic: This style of architecture, particularly church architecture, used in the later medieval period, originally developed in the 12th century. It replaced Romanesque. It is characterized by pointed arches and large expanses of stained glass.

keystone: This is the topmost block of stone in an arch, often picked out for decorative and symbolic purposes. It is sometimes taken to be the most important stone in the arch, but actually it would collapse if any one of them were to be removed.

Mock Tudor: a very popular English style that involves the notional evocation of the decorative effects of the timberwork that could be found in traditional timber-framed houses.

Modernism: 1. architecture inspired by the CIAM, characterized especially by its use of planar forms, non-traditional materials, avoidance of historical associations; often referred to as the Modern Movement, or in the USA as the International Style; 2. any architecture, especially of the mid-20th-century, that worked by experimental rather than traditional means; 3. architecture of the later 20th century and after that makes use of Modern Movement buildings as historical reference points.

naos: the Greek name for a cella; used as an English word when referring specifically to Greek temples.

Neoclassical: This is a version of classicism from the later 18th century that made use of specifically Greek and not Roman ideals of beauty. 'Neoclassical' is a 20th-century term. At the time the people involved called the style 'Grecian'.

Norman: This can refer to anything coming from Normandy, but in architecture it can be used as an alternative to 'Romanesque' when it is found in England: so called because the Romanesque spread rapidly through the kingdom after the Norman invasion of 1066.

order: In classical architecture the 'order' is the name given to the different types of columns, which bring with them a set of proportions not only for the column-type but also for the *frieze* and *entablature*, which varied from one order to another. See *Doric*.

pattern book: an illustrated book, designed to give architects and builders ideas to copy.

pediment: 1. the low sloping gable at the front of a classical temple; 2. a low sloping triangular form often placed to mark entrances or windows in classical buildings.

peristyle: a row of columns round the outside of a building, especially if the building is a classical temple.

portico: a porch with columns that takes the form of the end of a classical temple.

postmodernism: in architecture this term usually means a building from the 1980s that makes eccentric and unconventional use of historical ornamental features such as columns and keystones.

Regency: Properly this refers to the time between 1810 and 1820 when George III was King of England, but insane, so his son acted as the ruler (the regent). The son had an influence on fashionable taste over a longer period, from when he was Prince of Wales until he was George IV, and the 'Regency Style' would normally refer to this longer period. It is marked by simplicity and elegance of form (which is remarkable, given that the Prince Regent had built the Brighton

Pavilion). In contemporary popular usage with reference to architecture it suggests a rather notional indication of classicism.

Rococo: This was a late variant of the *Baroque*, which is different in mood, having a lighter touch. Its characteristic swirling plasterwork often used abstract or shell-like forms (*rocaille*) and delicate colour schemes.

Romanesque: This was medieval architecture, especially churches, built in imitation of Roman models, particularly architecture from the 12th century and before. It made use of round-headed arches and in the more ambitious work favoured stone-vaulted ceilings.

stoa: This was an ancient Greek building type with a long narrow rectangular plan. One of the long sides would have a wall along it, while the other would have a row of columns, leaving that side open to the outside. The arrangements made a pleasantly sheltered verandah-like space which was put to use in a multiplicity of ways. The most famous example was the *stoa poikile*, or painted stoa, in Athens, from which Zeno operated a school of philosophy (the Stoics).

vernacular: traditional buildings erected by craftsmen without the guidance of an architect.

Further reading

There are many different ways to look at architecture. The best way is to visit buildings and experience them. Reading about buildings makes sense most straightforwardly when one has visited them. Travel to the places illustrated in this very short introduction would give viable holiday destinations for years. Alternatively, take an interest in things close at hand, encouraged by a book such as Thom Gorst, *The Buildings Around Us* (Spon, 1995).

The following three volumes are concerned with architectural history, and order the material chronologically:

Sir Banister Fletcher, *A History of Architecture*, is an encyclopaedic volume that includes plans, line drawings and photographs of buildings of all ages and in all places. It is a very useful reference book and has been revised and reprinted many times since its first appearance in 1896. Earlier editions confined their scope to the Western tradition. It has changed under the influence of its various editors, and different editions have claimed the loyalty of different readers. The most recent edition, the twentieth, has 1840 pages and is called *Sir Banister Fletcher's 'A History of Architecture'*, edited by Dan Cruickshank, Andrew Saint, Kenneth Frampton and Peter Blundell-Jones (Architectural Press, 1996).

Spiro Kostof, *A History of Architecture: Settings and Rituals* (Oxford

University Press, second edition 1995). This illustrates fewer buildings, but across an equally wide range. The text offers more interpretation, and situates the buildings in their various cultures. It is widely admired and used in university courses.

David Watkin, *A History of Western Architecture* (Laurence King, third edition 2000) confines its scope to the Western tradition, stressing the continuity of that tradition in twentieth-century architecture. By excluding alternative viewpoints and perspectives, he simplifies matters and, partly as a consequence, the text is highly readable.

The idea of 'home' is the subject of a book by Witold Rybczynski: *Home: a Short History of an Idea* (Viking, 1986). It gives an impression of how our ways of occupying houses have changed over the centuries.

Michael Pollan, *A Place of My Own: the Education of an Amateur Builder* (Random House, 1997) describes the commissioning and construction of a small building in the author's garden, and shows how personal and emotional investments are made along with the effort and ingenuity involved in building.

The range of forces at work on buildings is explored in Edward Allen, *How Buildings Work* (Oxford University Press, second edition 1995). The books shows how many things find resolution in a building's design, and is complemented by Stewart Brand, *How Buildings Learn: What Happens After They're Built* (Viking, 1994) which shows how people adapt buildings to overcome problems that the designers did not anticipate.

There is a host of more specialized studies that caters to particular interests, and the bibliographies and recommendations in the books listed above will point towards them. A few historic texts can be recommended for the insight that they give into the architecture of different eras. The older they are, the more certain one can be that an untutored intuitive reaction to the text will be a misinterpretation. Nevertheless there is no substitute for reading them, to give an impression of the ideas that motivated architects in other ages. Ancient: Vitruvius, *Ten Books on Architecture*, translated by Morris Hickey Morgan (Harvard University Press, 1914 – reprinted and available in paperback) or by Ingrid Rowland (Cambridge University Press, 1999). Medieval: Suger's account of the works at Saint-Denis (available in translation edited by Erwin Panofsky, Princeton University Press, second edition 1979). Renaissance: Alberti, *On the Art of Building in Ten Books*, translated by Joseph Rykwert, Robert Tavernor and Neil Leach (MIT Press, 1988). Neoclassical: Marc-Antoine Laugier, *An Essay on Architecture*, translated by Wolfgang and Anni Herrmann (Hennessy and Ingalls, 1977). Modernism: Le Corbusier, *Towards a New Architecture*, translated by John Rodker (Architectural Press, 1927 many reprints).

Index

A

B

C

D

E

F

G

H

I

J

K

L

M

N

O

P

Q

W

Z

POSTSTRUCTURALISM

A Very Short Introduction

Catherine Belsey

Opening with a disagreement between Lewis Caroll's Alice and Humpty Dumpty over the question of meaning, this Very Short Introduction traces the key arguments that have led poststructuralists to challenge traditional theories of language and culture.

While Catherine Belsey discusses such well-known figures as Barthes, Foucault, and Lacan, as well as Kristeva, Lyotard and Zizek, she also draws pertinent examples from literature, art, film, and popular culture, including Shakespeare's sonnets and Toni Morrison's *Beloved*, Titian and Baz Luhrmann, to explore the poststructuralist account of what it means to be a human being.

'in short, this book is lucid, provocative, and fun to read'

Linda Hutcheon, University of Toronto

www.oup.co.uk/isbn/0-19-280180-5